CALL ME CRAZY,
BUT I'M HEARING GOD

Kim Clement

Destiny Image₀ Publishers, Inc.
P.O. Box 310
Shippensburg, PA 17257-0310

"Speaking to the Purposes of God for this Generation
and for the Generations to Come."

For Worldwide Distribution, Printed in the U.S.A.

ISBN 10: 0-7684-2494-1

ISBN 13: 978-0-7684-2494-2

This book and all other Destiny Image, Revival Press, MercyPlace, Fresh Bread, Destiny Image Fiction, and Treasure House books are available at Christian bookstores and distributors worldwide.

For a U.S. bookstore nearest you, call
1-800-722-6774.

For more information on foreign distributors, call
717-532-3040.

Or reach us on the Internet:
www.destinyimage.com

1 2 3 4 5 6 7 8 9 10 11 / 09 08 07

CALL ME CRAZY,
BUT I'M HEARING GOD

Acknowledgments

To God, my best friend, familiar neighbor, and the source of everything. Thank you for making this journey possible.

To the following choice people, sent by God and who made these adventures a testimony of who God is in our world:

To Jane, my wife, best friend, and partner for life; you know everything about me and this makes the truth so exciting because you were there from the start and have been a witness to God's working in my life. Without His "work" there is no "word"—you were there for the work as well as the word. Thank you.

To Donné, Jacquelyn, Caleb, Elizabeth, and Jakob, my children. You are the breath that I take everyday; without you there is no expression.

To Babette, my mother, who forced me to continue classical music until I was converted to Rock and then to The Rock, Christ Jesus. Thanks E.B. I'll keep the volume down when I retire.

To my late father, V.C. Your dream was for me to enjoy what I did one day—I love it! Your desire was always to have boys with short hair and neat appearances…sorry. Your labor and gentle strength paid off—we're all good fathers because of you. This is the real deal in Christendom and speaks more than the greatest sermons. Thank you for your example.

To the devil, for making God look so great.

To my dedicated team. A.T., Hannah, Miranda, Sunil, Charlie, Debbie, Johnny, Cindy, Velasco, Danny, Stan, and Joel—without you this prophetic voice would lack passion and energy. You are God's choice and what a choice!

To Don Milam for being a friend and placing pressure on me to make this project successful, and for enjoying fine wine with me.

To Angelina Snoots—you little flirt—only a year old and catching my attention constantly.

To the Warriors of God for standing on the sidelines encouraging me during difficult times—you're the partners that every minister dreams for. Thank you for your love and support.

To Bishop Dick Bernal. You're a friend not only to me and my household, but a friend of God. You believed in my style before many others did, and because of that I am free to be who I am today.

To David Clement, my brother. Thank you for believing in me and for remembering all the moments in my life that I had forgotten. There is a friend who sticks closer than a brother. You are both.

To Shelley Belton, my only sister. Your great mission in life—family. You are the invisible thread that holds us all together. Your smile and laugh, contagious even when you have pain, tells the depth of your character. We all need a dose of Shelley to remember the sanctity of family.

To my late brother, Barry. We will never forget you. You live in these pages because you were there before I was born and helped fashion a sound in me. Your trumpet is alive in me.

To my dear doctor and friend, Lance Wallnau. You have made me aware of my strengths, and you have been there to subdue me in the storms and fire me up in the calm. You are a genuine voice into my life.

God, I have a request: Let's do some more crazy stuff!

Contents

Foreword

I T brings me great pleasure to tell you about a man, his ministry, and this wonderful book. I have known Kim Clement and his family for more than 15 years. Without hesitation I must say that Kim has the most unique gift that my church, Jubilee Christian Center, or I have ever seen. Kim's prophetic insight and style of writing make it easy for the rest of us to better understand, "thus says the Lord."

When people ask me out of frustration, "Pastor, why isn't God speaking to me?" my answer is, "Maybe He is, but you're not listening with ears of discernment." Kim's gift helps us all look into the future with hope and excitement.

Back in the early '90s I was extremely frustrated over our building project. We had been leasing for years while Silicone Valley's land and building prices were soaring—it looked as if we would never fulfill our dream of building our sanctuary. Kim showed up and began prophesying, "I see three buildings... three...three," he kept shouting. My first reaction was "Three?" I barely had the faith to see one. Today we not only have three beautiful buildings on our campus but they are all paid for!

Recently Kim did it again. He sowed into our future and prophesied something huge for our ministry. No longer do I waiver at the prophetic word of the Lord.

This book will encourage you to hear the unthinkable, believe the impossible, and see your future.

—Dick Bernal
Pastor, Jubilee Christian Center
San Jose, California

Introduction

WHILE in Tampa, Florida, in the late 1990s, I met a man who quickly became a dear friend to me. I've been honored to be his friend for several years now and to be a spiritual influence in his life. His name is Peter Lowe, a phenomenal motivational speaker and minister. Through the years, Peter has been instrumental in introducing me to celebrities, politicians, past and present presidents, and great leaders. I have delivered inspirational revelations to many of them. Peter followed my predictions with great care and noted the depth of many of the predictions that I had given, particularly in the political and economical fields, where most spiritual leaders have become redundant.

He called me one day with a burden on his heart and said, "If I can arrange a meeting with Larry King, would you be prepared to meet with him?" I inquired as to the purpose of the meeting and he explained to me that he was frustrated that so many psychics were being interviewed and given exposure while God's prophets were basically ignored and never given the chance to be seen or heard. He thought it would be great if I could be interviewed along with a psychic. My first response was that I was not interested, as

I did not feel like dueling with psychics and such an encounter would only result in stone-throwing.

Peter left it at that; but over the course of a year, I felt that the Spirit wanted me to meet Larry King, if for no other purpose than to share a word from God with him. I contacted Peter and told him that I was prepared to meet Mr. King to see what kind of interview format he had in mind. I told him that I had received a prophetic insight for Mr. King and if the only reason for meeting was to deliver that word, it would be enough for me since I was not interested in any publicity.

Peter made the appointment and we met at Spago, in Beverly Hills. I found Mr. King to be a delightful man, and he immediately made me feel at ease. I delivered the prophecy that I had received and handed it to him in the form of a written scroll. During the course of the evening and after various questions, he said that he would have me on his show. He asked me about various predictions and, acting as the devil's advocate, he asked me difficult questions, provoking thoughtful answers.

One of the questions he asked: "Do you know where Saddam Hussein is?" I answered promptly, "If I did, I wouldn't be sharing it at this table." Oddly enough, since that meeting, I was honored to predict that during the Christmas season of that year, America would see the capture of Hussein and that he would be pulled out from his hiding place in a hole.

At one point, Mr. King asked me what the difference was between a psychic and a prophet. I thought for a moment and replied, "Psychics speak to the dead who are 'living'; prophets speak to the living who are 'dead.' Some people are walking and breathing in this world but in actual fact are spiritually dead." You only have one life to live on this earth—why should you have to wait until you have died before you can be reached?

As our dinner was drawing to a close, he looked at me and asked me how I earned money. I told him that we operated through the support of partners and our live shows. He asked if I had written a book, and I told him I was working on one entitled, *Call Me Crazy, But I'm Hearing God.* He loved the title and went on to say that he would like to see me make money as well and that he would consider the interview when the book was released. I was touched that he was concerned about my financial well-being, and so I was inspired to put pen to paper.

That was three years ago—I wasn't going to rush into writing about something as sacred as hearing God's voice. Months turned into years as I continued to write in depth about my experiences, recalling so many of the great moments that I have experienced during the 30 years that I have carried this gift. *Call Me Crazy* will make you realize that you are actually quite normal and that you could fit into the same category.

I'm not suffering from craziness—I'm enjoying every minute of it.

Join me,

—Kim Clement

Chapter 1

Why They Call Me Crazy

"WHY don't these people sleep?" I thought, listening to the sounds of Dixieland through the muffle of the wall. There was occasional shouting and singing; the sounds of the night in New Orleans are steeped in musical history. It was the sound that I had loved as a young man in South Africa, never dreaming that I would ever be part of it's future or that I would be walking the streets and seeing the reality of the jazz I had performed so many times, on so many different platforms.

In the late 19th century, as the rest of America stomped its feet to the military marches of war, New Orleans was dancing to Voodoo rhythms. New Orleans was the only place in the New World where slaves were allowed to own drums. Voodoo rituals were openly tolerated and well-attended by the rich and the poor, the Black and the White, and by the influential and the anonymous.

It was in New Orleans where the bright flash of European horns ran into the dark rumble of African drums—like lightning meeting thunder. It made people feel free and alive. It made people get up and dance, dancing to the birth of American music.

Everything about New Orleans, on the surface, seemed joyful and jubilant, and yet while I was lying in that hotel room trying to sleep, I was deeply disturbed. I was anxious and unsettled.

That night proved to be different in many ways. It was February 2005, and I had brought my family to be with me while I was performing in the city. For some reason they were all unhappy. Everyone was depressed. In particular, my wife, Jane, felt what she described as "death all around me." I had never heard her say anything like that before. She went on to describe herself as being severely depressed.

Why would she be depressed with all of this festive music? Everything in New Orleans is touched by the joyous anarchy called New Orleans Jazz, and everybody's middle name is "celebrate." It's perfectly clear that jazz began in New Orleans, and some of my heroes were in its foundation stones: Louis Armstrong, Sidney Bechet, Ellis Marsallis, Brandford Marsallis, Harry Connick, Jr., and the list goes on.

Eventually, I fell into a restless sleep but soon awoke to feel the room filled with something I can only describe as dark and devious. I got up, washed, and went into an area where I could pray. I opened the Manuscripts and read the words of life that had brought peace to me so many times. I sensed that in this room in New Orleans was a different kind of evil, and I shivered as I prayed for spiritual insight.

Death in the City

There was an unusual struggle over the next 24 hours, and I was constantly aware of the presence of death, something I had only experienced a few times in my life. Although I was battling these feelings, I somehow adjusted and searched for some kind of understanding from the Spirit. We performed that night, and what was normally easy for me to do, became strenuous. Communicating with the crowd was awkward, and the heavens seemed to be shut—I had no prophetic revelation. I looked out at the audience and no longer saw people but rather empty seats, and I felt a feeling of relinquishment, as if all spiritual authority had vacated the city.

Our dear friends, Garland and Beverly Bilbo, were hosting us while we there, and it now had come time to leave the great New Orleans. We were anxious to begin our journey back to Dallas, which is where we lived at the time. We climbed into our vehicles, and my wife, Jane, turned to all of us and said, "I need to get out of here; last night I had a nightmare about bodies coming out of the tombs and all I sense is death." I realized at that point that we were detecting a serious situation, and I needed my gift to offer some clarity.

As we were leaving, we entered the freeway barely outside of the city limits, and our vehicle got a flat tire. It was muggy and hot, so we called AAA to come change the tire for us. It took them an hour to reach us, and while they were changing the tire, I walked away from the vehicles and looked at the city. Suddenly a dark claw emerged slowly from the clouded sky and I thought, "We are struggling to get out of this city. The people of this city will also be fighting to leave, as we are now."

I turned to my manager and friend, A.T. Snoots, and mentioned this to him, "Something is stopping us from leaving this city. It's as if I'm experiencing this as a prophetic gesture because this is going to happen in the future."

As we left, I breathed a sigh of relief. I had experienced a swift current of spoken words and a dark depression, and I felt uneasy and perturbed. I lacked the sense of security that I normally felt after I had prophesied in a city. Something was wrong.

HOUSTON, TEXAS

On the evening of July 22, 2005, I was performing in Houston, Texas, and the crowd was alive. Everything was going beautifully, and the music was superb. The atmosphere was filled with positive and powerful spiritual energy. There was expectancy in the hearts of the people, which is always good for a prophet because celebration is the key to releasing the "word" from God. Someone once told me, "Kim, never go where you are tolerated; go where you are celebrated because it draws the best from your gift."

My friend, Garland Bilbo, had driven from New Orleans and was in attendance that night in Houston. While I was on the stage dealing with a subject entirely irrelevant to New Orleans or Garland, I was gripped by the same feeling that I had had when I saw a vision of planes flying over New York City, committing terrorist acts (World Trade Center Towers). I felt terror, and a great darkness came over me. I was no longer under my own control. Suddenly, the Spirit of God snapped me around, and I pointed at Garland, who represented New Orleans, and shouted out these words:

"O New Orleans, God speaks to you from Houston tonight and says, 'Enough of this! For a judgment is coming,' says the Spirit of the Lord, 'and I will take the men that have stood in faith, raise them above the flood that shall destroy those who constantly bicker and stand against My servant Moses, or My servant Bilbo. I want you to understand there are great men in New Orleans that have faith, but you have been set aside not to lose, but to win! Enough of this! For I will take the curses and the bodies will even rise and they will come forth on the water, but I will keep you, and the stench of death will only last a few days and then what I promised two years ago will come to pass for August, September, and October of this year. I made a promise it would happen.'"

I was stunned and shaken. This is not the kind of prediction I am acquainted with, and for me to go as far as speaking about death is highly unusual. I was now faced with the dilemma of explaining what this meant. The prophecy was a mixture of actual and spiritual events. Parts of the prophecy have a two-fold meaning. God promises that, *"He will take the men who have stood in faith and raise them above the flood that shall destroy those that constantly bicker and stand against my servant Moses"* (referring to any pioneering movement). The flood, in this instance, is spiritual, and as Isaiah, one of the Jewish prophets, said, "When the enemy comes in, like a flood the Spirit of the Lord will raise up a standard against him," meaning like a flood, God will come against the forces that speak against and oppose His will.

However, what God says next, *"For I will take the curses, and the bodies will even rise and they will come forth on the water,"* I believe, is referring to the actual flood. Evidently, the curses and the bodies are connected, dealing with ancient spirits. "*But I will keep you* (New Orleans)," meaning that New Orleans will not be completely annihilated, "*and the stench of death will only last a few days,*" I believe that this could be spiritual. This catastrophe did take place in August and the raging storms did continue through the summer, both physically and spiritually.

On Sunday, August 28, 2005, just before Hurricane Katrina hit, I felt the urge to play the audio version of the prophecy that I had given in Houston, at my meeting in Hollywood. At that point, the weather forecast for New Orleans was extremely ominous and foreboding. I asked the people to gather around the altar to pray for the historic city that was being threatened by Katrina. We prayed and asked God to pour His mercy on New Orleans.

After the raging storm passed, I looked back at what God told me about it before it happened, and I thought, "Now, *that* was crazy!"

CALL ME CRAZY

You may call me crazy, my own family and friends may call me crazy, and I may even call myself crazy at times. But crazy as it may be, when I hear God, it's the most exhilarating rush I've ever had in my life.

Sometimes I hear Him when there's music and lights and people cheering, sometimes it's over a quiet dinner or in the privacy of my studio where I love to pray and play my music. Sometimes I hear Him when I'm sitting on a plane, or while I'm watching a movie, or when I'm on live television with millions of people watching, waiting to see if I hear Him. It's all crazy; hearing from God has been crazy for thousands of years.

It seems like only the "crazy" people are the ones who hear Him, or so say the mass majority of people. Are we really crazy? Or are we just crazy enough to take a risk, to put our reputations on the line, giving our all to get the message we so strongly believe in across to the world?

Noah, the Jewish prophet Elijah, Joan of Arc, Martin Luther King, Jr., Abraham Lincoln, and so many more, were all crazy enough to hear from God. They called Noah crazy when he had never seen a drop of rain in his life, and yet he built an ark based on the only evidence he had—God's voice (see Gen. 6:9-22). They called the warrior Gideon crazy when he obeyed God and took 300 men with sticks and lamp stands to fight armies of tens of thousands (see Judg. 7).

They called Joan of Arc crazy when she acted on her visions from God and successfully helped recover her homeland from English domination. They called Martin Luther King, Jr. crazy when he said, "I have a dream." They called Jesus Christ crazy when He stood at the tomb of His friend Lazarus who had been dead for days, and told them to remove the stone from his tomb so Lazarus could come out (see John 11:1-46).

Call me crazy, but I'm hearing God. Do you hear him? Do they call you crazy? Or are you satisfied living with the attitude that as long as you're happy, why should you change anything? Why upset the apple cart? Maybe God wants to upset the cart because it's going a little too smoothly and something needs to fall.

HE *WANTS* TO SPEAK TO YOU

It's what He originally intended. He created man to have a friend *to talk to*. It's been His desire all along. Who wouldn't want to hear from God Almighty? Apparently, and unfortunately, a whole tribe of people didn't want to hear His voice. Even when the great Jewish leader Moses tried to encourage the people of Israel to listen to His voice, they remained at a distance from God. They didn't want to hear God for themselves and told Moses to *hear from God* on their behalf (see Exod. 20:18-19).

He had just brought them out of captivity from the Egyptians, leading them into freedom, supplying their every need, and then they do that! What a slap in the face for them to say they don't want to have any direct communication with Him. This gave God no choice but to raise up prophets, those who would celebrate in hearing from Him, people who would wait anxiously for yet another word. He chose people throughout the years that would not only *hear* Him, but who would allow Him to *speak through them* to the world. You can hear Him. He's speaking to you right now. All you have to do is listen.

If you're going to hear the voice of God, you're going to have to get acquainted with unreasonable dreaming, because God operates outside of the realm of reason. *Reason* is the power to form judgments by a process of logic. When you operate solely within this realm you are limiting your judgment to what is right and practical, what we like to call common sense. However, show me an example in the ancient manuscripts where logic accomplished something that had never been done before.

It is said, "prayer asks for rain, but faith takes the umbrella." I would like to go further by saying that when God reveals to you that it's going to rain, faith builds an ark. So big is your expectation, that you start building outside of reason. God told Noah to build an ark without a sign of rain—pretty unreasonable. Jesus told Peter to go fishing so that he could pay his tribute money to Caesar. Peter went and the first fish he caught had a silver coin in its mouth—pretty unreasonable (see Matt. 17:24-27). However, not only did it pay the taxes, but because Peter simply obeyed and acted, God performed something that had never, ever happened before. *God does not need to do the same thing twice.* Now, He may do the same thing over and over if He wishes, but it could be because He can't find anyone who will simply act upon His command.

Every person throughout history who heard God's voice and acted accordingly did something that had never been done before. Moses was told that he was to part the sea with a stick. Parting the sea is an unreasonable and impossible venture for any human being, so why would God choose a impossible method to perform an impossible feat? Simply because there is no possible, reasonable method to perform this kind of miracle. He chooses *His* methods, not ours.

REPETITION DULLS THE MIND, HEART, AND SPIRIT

American poet W.D. Snodgrass wrote: "If you're doing anything you know you can do, you're not doing anything at all."[1]

Human beings prefer to congregate in the halls of the known. History makes us feel safe, and, therefore, any new idea will immediately face skepticism and ridicule. But God will speak to any human being who *is* prepared to take a risk and be creative. To repeat the same thing over and over brings dullness to a people.

Take a look at music. Recently my daughter and her husband came over to my house for a barbecue, and while they were there, I noticed that they turned on music from the '70s. This was interesting to me, because they are young and from a generation who embraces rap and rock, etc. I inquired about this, and my son-in-law, John, said, "The music today is nothing but an attempt to reinvent the musical wheel of the '90s, and it's boring; so we listen to the music that came from pure creativity."

Today, the lack of creativity in music is causing man to be dull of hearing, and as a result, the words have become obscene, in most instances simply because once you reach a stalemate and you fear stepping into the unknown, man's evil human nature will vent his own personal feelings. Where are the Cole Porters, Muddy Waters, Beethovens, Beatles, Duke Ellingtons, and Paul Simons of today?

YOU ARE NOT A CLONE

Don't allow yourself to be defined by what you don't do. If we don't do what we were born to do, we relegate others to being the most brilliant minds in our generation.

You are an individual, not a religious clone. Genetic cloning is one of the ideas born in the synagogue of satan, the throne of religion. Religion is the organization that has structured everything so tightly, that it brings starvation to the imagination of millions of upright people, and undermines the creativity of the Spirit, offering nothing more than a repetition of what has previously been a success in their world.

To be prophetic in any way is an insult to their system, because they thrive on manipulating human beings with stories of achievements that came about by good works only. By doing this, they conform people into replicas of their leaders. The truth is, there is no defining of the terms laid down by the ancient manuscripts, the inspired Word of God. When it comes to dealing with the impossible, you must simply act on God's voice!

I've watched too many Christians take a "moment" that they've experienced with God and make it a fetish. Suddenly the experience is promoted to brand-new terms laid down so that everyone outside can experience the same wonderful moment. You dare not even attempt to work the same miracle outside of the principle laid down by the individual, who has become an artifact in a museum, a constant reminder of their past victory and an effort to *keep the burning bush burning*!

In our day and age, the burning bush encounter would've been commercialized and sold. Preachers would've taken trips to Mt. Sinai to pick up little sacks of ash. Books would've been written describing in great detail how God sounded, and how you could have the same burning bush experience…all for the small price of a sack of cloth. Remember, while God was speaking, the bush kept burning, but after He stopped speaking, the bush became a pile of ashes. Most people today would rather gather around the ashes and attempt to revive the bush *instead of follow His voice*. Moses had to follow God's voice into unreasonable places and situations. He did and they called him crazy.

EVERYTHING IN ITS TIME IS BEAUTIFUL...
(SEE ECCLES. 3:11)

A prophetic dream has to be given outside of its time, for obvious reasons. The dream comes to the chosen candidate, and usually it is blurry and unclear. But as time progresses, focus changes, and clarity sets in.

The following instances are achievements that came about because of a dream, outside of time, which proved to be beautiful in its own time:

- They called Galileo crazy when he looked through the telescope that he had perfected, and saw the planets and the universe, all part of God's creation, which were initially rejected by the church.
- They called Columbus crazy when he searched for support for his journey to a new world.
- Einstein was called crazy when he talked about the movement of light, which led to his theory of relativity.
- Robert Hutchings Goddard, known for launching the world's first liquid-fueled rocket, dreamed of reaching extreme altitudes and was called crazy. Goddard said, "Every vision is a joke until one man accomplishes it; once realized, it becomes commonplace."

It is never easy to act upon a "prompting" when you know it's going to cause havoc and controversy. If you want to live your life through the Spirit, then you will have to be led by His Spirit, not by your mind, emotions, or "fear of man."

There are some people who claim to hear God's voice and act/function *outside* of His revealed character. They are usually non-creative bigots who are bound by selfish motives. This is never God's voice, because God is love and will never hurt another human being. Remember that when the Spirit of God speaks to you, it will be defined by how He has acted in the past, and it can never be redefined by any human mind. That's why the Ancient Manuscript—the Bible—is our guide.

Jesus instructed us to "love your neighbor as yourself" (Matt. 22:39). It is important to understand that when God speaks to you, it's usually about you and how you're supposed to help people, or your family or friends; it's not for the purpose of interfering in another's well-being and personal life. The minute control becomes the motivational factor, you're not going to be called *crazy*—you are *crazy*.

I assure you that when God speaks to you, that day will be your last comfortable day on earth. But the comfort you lose is the repetitious, boring life that religion offers. Dead religion offers nothing else but the comforts of imaginative starvation. It starves the imagination. I want to provoke you to act and do something that has never been done before.

ENDNOTE

1.   William DeWitt Snodgrass, quoted on http://www.creativequeststudio.com/newsletter.html.

Chapter 2

The Sound of the Future

I could hear the sound of music in the distance, behind closed doors. The cold floorboard was my seat as I rested my back to the wall and stared up at the water-stained ceiling. My hands were moist, and my heart was racing. I turned to look at the other children surrounding me, and I knew that they were all feeling what I was feeling—absolute terror.

My musical training had always been intense, but today I was to be tested alongside children of varied ages. It was intimidating being so young. At the age of 8, I was dwarfed by most of the young talent that waited with me. We were not being judged based on age or seniority in this setting. Today, we sat there together, knowing the inevitable moment would present itself, the moment we were all dreading: *the test.*

Our musical ability would be tested on the grand, classical pieces of music that came from the passion and pain of the greatest musicians in history. Beethoven, Bach, Schubert, and Mozart were only a few of the composers whose music we were to perform and be judged on.

In order for all of us to be tested and graded, professors from London had come to conduct final exams. We had all been anxiously waiting outside the hall of a Catholic school in my hometown of Uitenhage, South Africa. As I watched students enter and exit through the huge wooden doors, I could feel the breeze from an open window, and the warmth of the morning sun. I knew that I would never forget this day. This was an interesting thought for such a young child, but it was imprinted inside of me, and I was overwhelmed as my heart drummed in my ears.

I looked down at the piece of music in front of me and it looked foreign to me. I had practiced this a thousand times, but fear overcame my mind. Some would call it stage fright.

"Master Clement, you are to be tested on your classical training at the 6th level. Please come with me." I don't know how I managed to stand up, because I couldn't even feel my legs. They must have been moving, because all I could hear was the clip clap of my shoes on the old floorboard as it creaked under my feet and bellowed in the huge empty hall. I tried to relax my mind and not think too much about what I was about to do.

Seconds that felt like hours brought me to face my judgment as the frail old man rose to his feet and stuck his bony, age-stained hand in my face. He said, "Master Clement, level 6 examination. Are you ready to begin?" I wanted to confess to him that I had no recollection of the music I had worked so hard to learn, but as I cleared my throat, the words that came out surprised both the professor and myself, "My hands are ready, but my mind is not." The professor hesitated for a moment and then clumsily asked if I needed a drink of water. I declined and turned to my instrument, the piano.

To test my skill at discerning a chord structure without watching what the examiner was playing, they conducted a test called the ear examination. I don't remember the test; I only remember suddenly feeling focused. The professor had been crouched over the piano as he played various notes and chords, all the while asking me to identify them without looking at what he was playing. After several minutes, I heard him whisper, "Impossible."

I had been standing with my back to him, but upon hearing his surprised whisper, I swung around. He stared at me with aged wisdom, a gaze that surely, in all its years, could see no more surprises; but there it was. His look was one of admiration and yes, surprise. "Your ear is perfect. I have never tested a student who could name each note that I play without a mistake. You have not missed a single note." He leaned back and a glimmer of doubt crossed his eyes, "I need to trick you to satisfy my own curiosity."

I turned back around in silence. The nerves and trembling returned as I realized that this was a test within a test. How much more of this could I endure? I closed my eyes and gave in to the moment.

After ten minutes of chords, single and double notes, low bass notes, and high treble notes, he abruptly stopped tinkering on the piano and walked toward the door, without a word to me.

I stood there, watching him leave, hoping that everything was all right, and wishing to be out of there and back in the comfort of my home. My mind drifted as I anxiously waited. I imagined myself before a crowd of people. I was playing and singing, and colored lights surrounded me on a dark stage. I couldn't quite imagine the music, but I saw my own hands, although they were older and decorated with a wedding ring, hammering the piano like a madman. Light beamed onto my face, and I could feel the sound…

I heard the door opening and was immediately pulled back into the present as the professor entered. He had performed in London since the early 1900s, and as I watched his aging body struggle to cross the huge room, I could see the way he would have walked as a youth. He was a maestro, a conductor of orchestras, and the dignity was evident in him. He stood in front of me and asked me to do some sight-reading.

I detested sight-reading; I would have to play a whole piece of music that I had never heard before, solely from reading the notes. They tested us this way to see if we had the ability to interpret the notes and perform them without prior study or practice. I stared at the piece of music in front of me as I sat at the piano. I tried to play, but was unable to read it. I had failed miserably, but this was not the end of the test.

The professor stopped me and then told me to do something that was both unorthodox and outside of his duty as the examiner of an 8-year-old boy. "Give me your sheet music." With trembling hand, I gave it to him. "Now play the piece, if you can remember it," he continued.

Suddenly, something woke up inside of my being, and I began to play. I played the entire piece from memory, forgetting about the test and the examining professor. I no longer felt the stress of the day, I felt connected to this feeling as I played. I played with my eyes closed and my head raised. I finished the piece and turned to look at the professor who was staring down at his grading papers. It was evident that he was both moved and bewildered by what he had just seen and heard.

He stood to his feet and asked me to open the music that I had practiced for this day so that he could complete the exam and give me my grade. The pieces that I had practiced totaled 28 pages, and even though I had practiced and practiced, I still could not perform them without the direction of the sheet music. I regained my composure, and tried to read the music as I began to play.

I turned the page, and then the next page, all the while playing the piece perfectly. Suddenly the professor bellowed, "Stop!" Shocked at this sudden outburst, I jerked my hands from the piano and stared straight ahead of me. I looked at his reflection in the finely shined wooden piano as he approached. "I am looking at the same piece of music that you are performing, but you are not turning the pages at the right time. You are not reading this music, you are playing it from memory, and you are playing it perfectly!"

I could not think of an answer and stared up at him in confusion and fear. I was a child, and I had no idea how I was doing it. I stood and waited while the professor explained to my teacher that he was unable to evaluate me properly, due to the strange features in me that he could not explain. He suggested a second examiner, and they released me with an incompletion. This was my first encounter with the supernatural. This was my first glimpse into the strange, difficult, and unique life that I was about to live.

DEVELOPING THE SOUND

I was born in Uitenhage, a little town in South Africa near the city of Port Elizabeth in the Eastern Cape Province. I had a normal

South African home and upbringing. I was the second son of Vyvian and Babette Clement.

My parents had a great love for classical music and dreamed that (at least) one of their four children would be a great classical musician. For this reason, all four of us were musically trained from a very early age. I had two brothers, my older brother Barry and my younger brother David, and one beautiful little sister, Shelly. Each of us had our instrument, and mine was the piano.

We occasionally went to church, but we only vaguely remembered the Bible stories we heard there, and we never put much thought into them and what they meant. I remember actually being expelled from the Children's Church, and after that, my mother told me I didn't have to attend anymore. Other than the occasional funeral and wedding, that was the extent of the church experience in our lives.

I began my musical journey at the age of five in the hands of my Aunty Belle. A few times a week, I would walk the short distance from my house to hers for lessons. I remember the musty smell of her old house, where she lived with her husband, Walter. Stained glass windows, old wooden floors, and a long dining room table comprised my classroom; and I remember the piano.

Aunty Belle was quite a character, with a great love for music. She was also very hard on me as she taught me the discipline necessary to embrace my talent. If I ever made a mistake, she would smack my knuckles with her long pencil. It would sting my hands, and the cold of the room would worsen the pain; however, I would suck up my feelings of anger and persevere. "You're not catching a train, slow down!" she would yell, as I nervously tried to finish my lesson.

While still studying with Aunty Belle, I was enrolled in our local branch of the Trinity Music College of London. I was forced to practice my music lessons for two or three hours a day. As you can imagine, this was very difficult for me to do at such a young age.

My mother had put all four of her children in musical training of some kind. Many times, against my will, my mother would make me perform for her friends and at various social events. I hated being a showpiece and resented having to perform to delight people I hardly knew.

However, as I grew as a person and musician, I began to dream of becoming famous for my musical ability. I would fantasize that I was performing for huge crowds all over the world, and I wanted to step into that future.

By the time I was ten years old, I had reached a point where I was excited to practice and perform. I wanted to do it and no longer felt uncomfortable when my mother would ask me to play for her guests.

It was around this time in my life, when my mother and I were out running errands in town one day. I was tired and impatient as I followed her around. Her crisp accent pierced my ears, "Come on Kim!" When she said my name, it sounded more like "Keem," which is now a comforting sound, but as a child I still wanted to run and play, and that voice meant that I would have to continue on the tedious journey through the fabric store. We were there purchasing fabric for my costume for the school play.

Upon leaving the fabric store, my mother took me to an apartment in our little town where a woman resided who claimed psychic powers. During our visit, the psychic took my hand and did a "reading." She told me that I would travel overseas as a musician and that I would become famous. My inhibitions were removed by her flattery. I listened with wonderment as she portrayed exactly what I had dreamed of becoming. I was a little fearful, yet intrigued by the mystical atmosphere.

We left with nothing much to say, although I imagine the advice of the clairvoyant was taken to heart by my mother, who leaned toward this kind of spiritualism. For me, this experience opened my eyes to a supernatural world that I had not sensed in the few church trips I had made in my short life.

A VOICE FROM ANOTHER WORLD

I remember something remarkable that happened to me when I was 11 years old. I was running and playing during lunch break at school with all the other kids. As I moved through the crowd, I was stunned by a sudden whisper in my ear, *"Duck!"* I immediately responded, and dropped to the ground, in front of a tree. At that moment, I heard someone scream as an object flew over my head and collided with the tree.

A few days earlier, a known bully had decided to pick on me and kicked me in the groin in front of the other kids, which was humiliating and painful for me. As I looked to see what the object was that was coming at me, I realized it was the very same bully, and he had been running toward me at full speed with every intention of tackling me to the ground. Unfortunately for him, he missed me and crashed into the tree. Stunned, bruised, and humbled, he walked away. I stood up feeling a bit strange and surprised, probably more confused than he was.

The word I heard was clear, audible, and I responded immediately, without any hesitation. A voice from another world had just warned me and acted as an intervention in what could have caused me unnecessary pain and conflict. I believe all of this was preparing me for future occurrences when an intervention would be necessary, but on a much larger scale.

A few days later, I was unexpectedly prompted to do something that seemed very strange to me. I requested that the wind would increase in force and volume. Instantly, the wind began to howl, and the dirt at my feet gathered into a whirlwind that was spinning around with incredible force. I covered my eyes and within seconds the wind died down.

LISTEN TO THE WIND

Though I knew nothing about God at that point, I knew this was no coincidence. I was intrigued, and I continued walking and pondering these events. Suddenly I felt an urge to just stop and listen. I waited, and as the wind began to gently blow, I heard the voice again. It said, *"Listen."* I stopped and strained to listen, but I heard nothing. *"Listen to the wind."* This time I stopped trying so hard to *hear*, and just *listened*.

For a moment, I was able to "see" (perceive) something that surpassed my natural abilities of sight and hearing. What I saw was an old castle. It was grey and majestic, and I could hear the shouts of people coming from within its walls. They were shouting as if they had just won a tremendous victory in battle. As I tell this story now, I still get chills remembering that moment.

The feelings that accompanied that experience are special and unique, and they've happened to me many times since that day. When that feeling comes to me, I know I'm about to hear from my Friend. I don't hold any delusions of grandeur about my ability to control the wind, but this is just one occurrence of many that have led me to believe that God moves in mysterious ways, seeking for an occasion to communicate with us. All He needs is someone who will take the time to listen and respond.

I had quite a few strange, psychic experiences in my early years. I didn't know at the time, but now I believe this was the gift at work in me even as a child. The gift was being formed in me, especially in my passion to express through music.

In that same year, I had an idea to start my own band. One day the doorbell rang at our house, and I ran to answer it. A gentleman stood before me and asked for my father. He was looking for Kim Clement in response to an ad I had placed in the newspaper for a band member audition. "I am Kim Clement," I said. I could tell that he didn't believe me. I was, after all, only 11 years old, and I'm sure he thought I was just a naughty kid teasing him.

I invited him inside and explained that I had placed the ad, and that I was the person looking for a band member. He was still not convinced, so I brought him over to our old upright piano, and began to play a few lines from the famous song "Puppet On a String," as if I was the one auditioning. His look of doubt melted into one of approval and excitement. He good-humoredly told me he thought the audition went great! He became the lead guitarist and manager in my band, Mark IV. Soon, we were booked in all the local nightclubs and becoming more and more popular. We even won several awards and were featured in one of the major local newspapers.

FINDING GOD IN THE SOUND

Around that same time, my brother and I were messing around running up and down through the attic entry in our bedroom. My older brother, Barry, was much stronger and bigger than I, and in all the fuss, I fell through the opening and crashed through the closet doors. I was overwhelmed by intense pain in my hip and back and had to just lie there until my brother could help me get to the bed. We hid the whole incident from our parents because we knew we'd probably get in trouble for being in the attic, especially if they knew it caused me to get hurt.

The next day, I was walking to school and suddenly the pain was so intense I doubled over and could barely put one foot in front of the other. Strangely enough, this was the same pathway I was on when I had the experience with the wind. To this day I can see it so clearly in my mind. I made my way slowly and painfully to school. When I arrived, they immediately contacted my parents to come and collect me and suggested that I be taken to the doctor immediately. I was taken to the hospital, and they confirmed that I had damaged my hip. I stayed in the hospital for the next three months. This was extremely frustrating for me, not only for the obvious reason of being a child confined in a hospital bed, but also because I had no way to play my music, and this sent me into depression.

One day, as I lay in the hospital bed, an Anglican clergyman came into my hospital room. I looked up as he approached. He was dressed in dark pants and a dark shirt, and I recognized that he was religious by the little white square peeking out of his collar. His smile was warm as he seated himself beside my bed. "Would you like me to pray with you?"

"No," I said. "I don't want any prayer." He looked me straight in the eyes and said, "Jesus still walks the streets today, and one day you are going to need Him. If you call on Him, He'll walk over to you, and He will touch you."

I had never heard anyone speak this way. I turned my head as he left the room, without letting him know that I was intrigued. These words would come back to me at the most important moment of my life.

I spent my teenage years as typical musicians did in the '70s. I had experimented with drugs like marijuana by the age of 12. At 14, I would ride the train to school with a fat cigar in my mouth. By the time I was 17 years old, I was addicted to heroin and obsessed with the heavy rock and roll music that was taking over our generation. Artists like Alice Cooper, Led Zeppelin, Jethro Tull, and Deep Purple were my idols.

TURNING POINT

I was 17 and had just played at a club in Port Elizabeth. I had been shooting heroin in the bathroom after my show. I must have passed out from the effects of the drug, but I was abruptly sobered when I felt what I thought was someone punching me in my shoulder. I looked around but only saw the shadow of a man leaving through the bathroom door. Suddenly, I realized that I was covered in blood! My mind was in a deep, dark fog as I struggled to gather my thoughts.

I stood up and saw my reflection in the mirror. At that moment, I saw that I had been stabbed near my shoulder and was bleeding profusely.

"I'm only seventeen, and I'm dying," I thought, as I pressed my hands against my chest in a desperate attempt to stop the flow of blood. "Isn't anyone going to help me?" I cried. No one heard me. I was alone.

I fumbled out of the bathroom, trying to find my way to the exit. I thought to myself, "Everybody here knows me, but nobody cares!" They say your life flashes before your eyes when you are faced with death; the life that flashed before me was meaningless and empty. I was living a life filled with hopelessness and despair. Nothing I was doing to bring me joy, and excitement was filling the deep emptiness that was now so evident to me. The drugs, alcohol, and rock star life were really only bringing me pain and bitterness.

I had attempted suicide that same month and suffered severe self-inflicted wounds. The strange thing about it is the area of my body I chose to inflict—my eye. One night I took the mouthpiece from my brother's trumpet and started gouging out my eye. It caused such trauma to my eye that my eyeball actually moved. To this day, I have vision problems caused from that fit of rage.

When I think about it now, I see how even then, the forces against me were trying to destroy my sight. How ironic that I was mentally prepared to take my own life, but now that someone else was trying to harm me, I was fighting to live. My successes as a rock star and musician meant nothing now as I fought for my life. I was in the process of scoring music for an Australian movie, but none of that mattered now, as I staggered along the street, wounded, and eventually dropping to the ground in despair. I was simply a man, overdosed on a powerful drug, bleeding to death alone in an alley.

Suddenly the words of the Anglican minister who had visited me in the hospital several years before began to echo in my mind: "Jesus still walks the streets today, and one day you are going to need Him. If you call on Him, He'll walk over to you, and He will touch you."

I realized this was probably my last chance, and I cried out in despair, "Jesus, if You are still walking the streets, come over to me now."

At that very moment, someone walked over to me, and like the Good Samaritan, he picked me up, put me in his car, and drove me to the hospital. He became the hands and voice of God to me.

As they were treating my wounds, I was going in and out of consciousness, mainly from the pain but also from the large amount of drugs in my bloodstream. I don't remember anything that happened during the next three days. When I woke up, the compassionate stranger was sitting by my bed, waiting for me.

When I was discharged from the hospital, he drove me to a friend's home where I could recover. I was still in terrible pain, and going through unimaginable, nightmarish withdrawals from the drugs. My body needed them.

The man said, "I want to tell you about my best friend. His name is Jesus." I don't know if I even realized, at that stage, that what this man was offering me was the very thing that I had cried out for. For the next few hours he shared the story of Jesus with me. Like a sponge, I absorbed everything he had to say. I knew nothing about this Man Jesus that he was telling me about, and I was fascinated with what I heard.

He said, "Jesus is here right now. He wants to touch you." He prayed with me, and I spoke my first words to this unknown Jesus, who was once a stranger to me but now would become my best friend. It was truly the most amazing experience of my life. Jesus saved my life. Therefore, from that moment forward, I dedicated my life to Him and His purpose for me on this earth.

Everything changed in my life after that, and since that day, I have been privileged to inspire hundreds of thousands of people around the world through my music and voice. I have never grown tired of it or considered it a burden. Although, at times, it has required sacrifice, the reward is far greater. I have never taken for granted this wonderful gift given to me.

Welcome to the Prophethood!

I began to discover this new sound, this prophetic sound that gave me the ability to see deep into the soul of the person before me. Unlike a psychic, I was seeing the root of their problems, the source of their pain, and with God's help, I was able to see them in the future, free of their heartache and exactly the way He intended them to be.

Since then, God has used my expression of music to unite the hearts of people, create a prophetic atmosphere, and trigger inspiring words from His heart to individuals and to nations.

Many religious churches, movements, and leaders have scowled at my style and method of communication (and often mocked it) due to the fact that it is not read correctly from the musical score or performed according to acceptable religious protocol. However, it is something that I cannot operate without. I am criticized severely by many individuals who know absolutely nothing about my life, my heart, and my history and relationship with God, and quite honestly, I couldn't be bothered.

I continue to breathe the air of inspiration, and I am nourished by the future. I am not moved by the applause of man. My journey has been exciting, surprising, painful, joyful, and mysterious. There is no passion without pain. Sometimes *my most notable* days are shadowed into nights, but my piano strings remain unrusted and my eyes are filled with light; at the end of the day, my heart is unclaimed by the disdain of men. I have endured much and I am passionate about my journey as a prophet. I choose to follow His voice wherever that may lead. Will you join me on my journey?

Chapter 3

The Journey of a Prophet

IT was a cold Texas winter in November 1993, and I was enjoying a day at home with my 13-year-old daughter, Donné. We had just recently made the difficult move from South Africa, knowing we were destined to live in the United States. It was definitely a sacrifice, especially for our children who had lived their entire lives in South Africa, surrounded by family and friends. The cultural change had been an adjustment, especially for Donné who was older and felt the effects of the move more strongly.

I had just spoiled my kids with two motorized scooters that reached speeds of 25 mph. They loved to ride them around the neighborhood and would always ask me to join them, so I decided to experience one of these speed racers myself. Donné had been riding around for a while, and as she rounded the cul-de-sac, she yelled out a challenge for me to race her.

I laughed but accepted the challenge. We started at the end of the driveway and off we went. The wind was cold as we rode around the block. I had been in the lead most of the way, but as we neared our street, Donné cut in front of me and around the corner. "Little sneak attack," I thought and accelerated to a higher speed.

As I sped past our mailbox, I squeezed the brake, but I wasn't slowing down! My heart raced as I hit the red emergency cut off button, but it didn't work. To my horror, I realized that the accelerator was stuck and I was heading straight for the enormous RV parked in my driveway. I had to think quickly. I knew I couldn't drive directly into the RV at 25 mph without killing myself, so my instinct kicked in, and I stuck my leg out in a last desperate attempt to stop. All I remember is the world spinning around me and my daughter's scream.

The next thing I knew, I was sitting on my driveway in excruciating pain. I grabbed my hand and realized that it was broken, and then the pain in my other hand told me that both of my hands were broken. I was in shock and in and out of consciousness as my wife led me into the house. I lay down on a bench in the kitchen as she grabbed the car keys. She had called 911 but didn't want to wait for them. She ushered me to the car and rushed me to the hospital.

Three surgeons came in to examine me and to give their professional opinion about the extent of the damage to my hands and wrists and what actions needed to be taken next. As I was falling, I stuck both of my hands out as I fell head first into the hard, grey concrete. Unfortunately, when I fell I didn't land on the palms of my hands. My hands folded forward and twisted upon impact, and all of my fingers and both wrists were broken. My right hand had broken off completely, under the skin, and I had actually been holding it onto my arm as I was rushed to the hospital.

The surgeons would have to operate immediately, and because of the kind of break in my wrists, they were going to have to use pins and plates to restructure my hands and wrists. They told me that once the pins and plates were in place, I would never perform on the piano the way that I used to and that I would always be greatly restricted.

This was the worst news I had ever received. My heart was sinking as they wheeled me into surgery. How could this be? After everything I'd been through in my life, this was the most unexpected and disappointing moment, to say the least. They did their best to correct the damage to my hands and wrists, but after I came out of the first surgery, I was informed that I needed another surgery.

The following day, they performed another surgery, placing a pin in my one wrist and a plate in my other. They released me and sent me home with medication for the pain. That night, I found myself pinned to my bed in the early hours of the morning in tremendous pain, so I reached out for the medication that I had been given by the doctors. I didn't know at the time, but I was severely allergic to the medication they gave me, and a few minutes after I had taken it, I stopped breathing and realized that I could very possibly be dying. I attempted to reach out for Jane, but my body was paralyzed. I began to shout, but because I couldn't breathe, I was unable to vocalize anything.

I panicked, and then suddenly heard a loud voice that seemed to be speaking into my skull because my head began to shudder. The voice tauntingly said, "So you will be piercing the darkness?" At that stage, I thought I had suffered a stroke, but with all the strength within me, I screamed out "Yes!" and I began breathing again. I fell off the bed and began weeping, in fear, confusion, and physical shock. I shook for an hour after that and then began vomiting. I vomited for six hours, and then dry heaving and a migraine emerged. It was the worst day of my life. By the end of the day, I was simply lying on the ground in agonizing pain, with casts on both my arms. I was so very weak. Was I really that evil that God would allow me to go through this? I asked Jane to pray for me as I was too weak to pray, and she did.

Over the next few days, I began seeing things beyond the year 2000. For five hours in the night, I had visions of so many things; and then, finally, I saw a company of young people, and when they shouted, they sounded like people going to war. I saw them wounded, even though they were young, but they were radical, revolutionary, and non-religious. Suddenly, I heard God speak to me, and He said, "You are seeing a generation of prophets who will emerge from the dust and become an army; Kim, your associates and friends will turn their backs on you, and you will be alone, but after a decade they will return to you—do not concern yourself about this; now give up your present ministry, take up your cross, and follow me. I am sending you to Detroit to recover, be restored, and to raise up your leaders."

After this, I stood up, and something had changed in me. I was ready to give it all up and start a new journey. I had been ministering since 1976 and was becoming popular in the United States in large churches. After traveling and struggling through the '80s, I had finally reached the place where my ministry would take off and affect many lives, and now God was telling me to bury it. Something in me died that day, and I asked God where to start. The next thing that happened to me was what we call the "contradiction to the prophecy." When God speaks to you like He did to me that day, the enemy of your soul immediately tries to come in and steal your joy and inspiration.

During my recovery period, I sought help and advice from my associates and friends in the ministry; what resulted was the straw that broke the camel's back. I was informed by some of these "friends" that my accident had been a punishment by God and that I needed to repent. I called these men over to my house, and during the confrontation, I fell on my knees, while still in pain from surgeries and with casts on both my arms, and asked God to forgive me for whatever I was guilty of. While praying, these men informed me that it was because my music was "worldly, ungodly sounding, and new age" and that I was to change my style of music immediately and conduct soft, gentle worship. I remained on my knees, and even though I was beginning to doubt that this was the cause, I agreed and prayed a prayer of sorrow.

CONFRONTING THE POWER OF RELIGION

Several weeks later, I received a letter in the mail from these ministers informing me that my repentance was not adequate and that I should go through the procedure again. I couldn't believe what I was reading, although it was something I was all too familiar with from years of being told what to do. This was religion speaking yet again. The most effective tool in satan's hand is the power of religion. Religion will try and keep you quiet and controlled, never allowing you to become the instrument God created you to be. You see, when I was introduced to Jesus, I came off the street and had no idea about Christianity.

My first day to church I walked in with long hair and a cigarette in my mouth. I had no clue about what I was stepping into. When I was filled with the Spirit, it was the most wonderful and beautiful experience for me. Then, when I tasted of the religious control, I was so disappointed because I realized that there was an aspect of Christianity that I never knew existed. It made something out of me that I didn't want to be, and it pulled me to pieces.

I had to learn a whole new language in order to fit in and sound like a Christian; I call it "Christianese." I was told to cut my hair and get rid of my cigarette, or I was not welcome there. I complied, eager to do anything to please my new best friend, Jesus. I followed all the requests of my pastor. I cleaned the church. I attended every prayer service, special event, and picnic that the church was hosting. But it didn't take me long to get close enough to Jesus to realize that He didn't care one bit about what I looked like or sounded like. As I was promoted, so to speak, in the church, I went from cleaning the toilets to playing the piano and speaking to the youth.

I began to gain a bit of confidence, and I was ready for ministry. I spoke exactly as they taught me to speak, sang all the songs they told me to sing, and did all the right things, but deep down I was screaming to do what I'm doing today. They handed me a Jimmy Swaggart record and told me that that was what I should be playing. There is nothing wrong with Jimmy Swaggart's music, but when you've been acquainted with the music of Deep Purple and Led Zeppelin, it's a little difficult to try to adjust and conform to a completely different style of music, while being told that the style you've loved and played all your life is wrong.

I hated what they were making me do and who they were try-ing to mold me to be. For years I complied with their structure and rules, never feeling like I was being myself. So when these men told me God was punishing me because my expression had become ungodly and worldly, I could take no more. Religion would no longer dictate my future.

This was a turning point in my life, and it changed my whole expression. When God spoke to me through the visions in the night, I saw the ones I call the Warriors of the New Millennium. I saw those who would shake the nations far into the New Millennium. I remember thinking, "But this doesn't line up with my eschatology." I believed that Jesus Christ would be returning before the New Millennium and therefore my vision was somehow blocked beyond the year 2000. That's the power of the religious control I was under, so much so that I couldn't believe the visions I was seeing beyond the year 2000. Your doctrine, creed and eschatology, if incorrect, will blind you to the future.

Nevertheless, God showed me those who were the prophets and leaders of this generation, covered with tattoos and pierced body parts. The enemy had done everything in his power to stop me that day, but I came back with a fresh and new sound. God told me to take up my cross and follow Him. I thought I was already doing that, but He said, "Kim, I want you to be who I created you to be before you were born." I threw away my uncomfortable suits and the ties that were choking me, and I honestly felt like I could breathe for the first time.

I tried to share what God had shown me with my associates and friends. I told them that I would be speaking and prophesying to presidents, and that our gatherings would be broadcast throughout the earth to millions of people, and that a different style of interactive ministry would draw the reprobates and dark souls into God's world of freedom. Their response was almost soul-destroying; they laughed at me, and they dug into my personal life and contacted ministry organizations warning them that they were dealing with an apostate and heretic minister and advising them to close their doors to me. My heart was broken, but the pain gave me the passion I needed to persevere to the next stage of my life.

OFF TO DETROIT

It took three months before I could even attempt to play the piano again, and when I did, I experienced excruciating pain. But I defied the words of the surgeons and pushed myself by playing every day. I began to prophesy on the piano and minister with my music in a brand-new way. The surgeons were right when they said that I would never play the piano like I did before, I played even better!

I came back with a vengeance and with an attitude that I knew was pleasing to God. Many friends and associate ministers had rejected and betrayed me. I had been wounded physically and emotionally. That's when I felt the call to Detroit. After being severely beaten down for years by the religious system because I could never conform to the style and status of the so-called minister, I needed a place where I could hide away while developing this new sound.

I knew nobody in Detroit but was soon introduced to a man who would become a close and faithful friend. Pastor C.L. Johnston, an older man with not an ounce of soul in him, was patient, kind, and open to the prophetic. Over the years, he not only facilitated my expression, but in seeing how weary I had become after the accusations from my own, he encouraged me and built a platform where I could be myself, without any religious restrictions.

When I saw him, I certainly didn't feel that he would be the appropriate candidate for me to team up with, given my culture, style, and the nature of my expression. However, when I approached him and told him that I was giving up my annual itinerary and that I was instructed by God to operate in Detroit for a season until I felt released, he seemed open to this, and offered me his building in Southgate, for what we would call our G.O.D. (Gathering of the Dangerous) meetings.

These gatherings were popular in the beginning, but eventually our crowds got smaller, and I realized that God wanted me with a faithful few, as I was being prepared for what would take place years later in Hollywood through the media. It was in Detroit where my expression was formed, and I raised up a team that would join me in inspiring the hearer and shaking the kingdoms of hell. We gathered the Warriors of the New Millennium and the Kick Devil Butt Generation, as they emerged from their caves. A new sound was born, and a generation was given another chance. Detroit brought the best out of me, and still to this day, when I go there, I feel so celebrated and protected. Some of my most creative musical pieces are born in Motown.

9-11 PROPHECY

Probably the most profound event that came out of our gatherings in Detroit was when I prophesied about a terrorist attack on

New York City. We had arranged a special week-long event called *The Gathering of the Dangerous* at the Hyatt Regency Hotel in Dearborn, a city just outside of Detroit, Michigan, with the largest Arabic population in the United States. The concept of the event theme was: if you've been wounded by your enemy (religion), but not enough to kill you, then your enemy better watch out because you are more dangerous to him now than you were before he tried to hurt you. Therefore, we gathered together the wounded and hopeless, and we inspired them to live their lives as God intended, no longer under the dictation of whatever was holding them down.

It was July 25, 1996, and a crowd of approximately 800 people were on their feet as I led them together in musical proclamations like, "We're gonna reach the unreachable and touch the untouchable!" Coincidentally, Bob Dole was speaking in the room next door to where we were meeting. All of a sudden, I was gripped with this overwhelming feeling of pain and loss as I began to see this picture unfolding in my mind of planes over New York City.

That was five years before America suffered the greatest terrorist attack in its history on September 11, 2001. That specific prophecy has unfolded in entirety.

TERRORIST PLOT THWARTED

In 1996, I heard these words, *"Even though you've been attacked, even though there's been terrorist attacks against you in planes* (collectively speaking of the various planes in the 9-11 attack), *and it's going to happen again, do not worry about it! The next time there will be a divine protection on that terrorist attack."*

Exactly 10 years after I gave the prophecy above, the last part of the prediction was fulfilled: *The next time there will be a divine protection on that terrorist attack."*

Just before the plot to blow up planes in flight from London to LAX (Los Angeles airport) was exposed, I started feeling something again and the following prophecies were an indication that something was happening in Great Britain and in the United States, specifically at LAX.

On July 8, 2006, at one of our Secrets meetings in Hollywood, I delivered this prophecy:

> *Rejoice because your prayers are destroying the power and the influence that shall endeavor to be sent to the L.A. Airport of this place, says the Lord. For God says, they are planning already. For they say, it is an easy target. It is easy access. They are cleaning it up. But the LAX Airport and, God said, those surrounding regions have been targeted with something very stupid, because they do not understand that the **saints of the Most High God** have been praying. And because they've been praying, God says, I will once again take them and expose them as I did in Florida. I will expose them on the West Coast and I will expose them over and over through the summer months as I promised you, says the Lord...."*

On July 29, 2006, in Detroit, Michigan I went on to say that, "*A lion will roar. A lion will roar from Great Britain. Something shall change, a drastic thing shall happen. And greater shall be the unity of the nations that shall gather around and say that it must be brought to an end now. This is the summer, the one that I promised.*"

On August 10, 2006, the BBC news announced that: "*A plot to blow up planes in flight from the UK to the US and commit 'mass murder on an unimaginable scale' has been disrupted, Scotland Yard has said. It is thought the plan was to detonate explosive devices smuggled in hand luggage on to as many as 10 aircraft.*"[1]

John Reid, the UK Home Secretary elaborated, saying they believed the "main players" were accounted for...." Reid went on to say that if the attack had been carried out, it would have caused the loss of life of "unprecedented scale." He concluded by saying that they were "confident" the main players were in custody...."[2]

On the same day in the United States, MSNBC reported that the terrorist plot was to simultaneously blow up 10 aircraft heading to the U.S. using explosives smuggled in hand luggage, averting what police described as "mass murder on an unimaginable scale."[3]

You will notice that the same wording that was used in my 1996 prophecy regarding the terrorist attack was used in describing the surroundings of this next terrorist attack. In the 1996 prophecy God said, "The saints of the most High God *will* pray" but in this specific prophecy, He says, "The saints of the Most High God *have been praying*" and therefore the attack was disrupted. This means that the time was drawing near for the fulfillment of the 1996 prophecy, but this time there was divine protection because people were praying. *Prayer does not change things; prayer changes you and you change things.*

The prediction also spoke of striking down the "God of the East," meaning spiritual influences over the Middle East. I also spoke of the "Kings of the East, the Prince of the East, the one who wages war against America," which I believe refers to Saddam

Hussein. Before 9-11-2001, in fact five years before, Saddam Hussein was tied into the terrorist attacks and has subsequently been brought down.

As a prophet, I personally don't care about who is in political power, but I believe that what President George W. Bush has done is more than just "gone to war" for God's sake. He is conducting a war against a powerful force, the "God of the East." This isn't something that can be handled with weapons of war but a spirit of war. According to His words, "The saints of the Most High God will begin to pray," prayer makes a difference. Elizabeth Elliot wrote, "Prayer lays hold of God's plan and becomes the link between His will and it's accomplishments on Earth."

It's been an interesting journey, to say the least. Since 2004, I have received letters from the previous associates and friends who had hurt me, apologizing and asking for reconciliation, and I have acted appropriately. The visions that I saw in 1993 have unfolded before my very eyes. Since then, I have indeed spoken to three presidents, prophesied to them, and given spiritual advice; and today our gatherings are broadcast in over 25 countries with a viewing audience of over 80 million people; our Website has drawn so much interest that we have more than 15 million hits a month. I have ministered to the reprobate, the pauper, and some of the darkest souls on the earth, and they are coming out of their caves to hear what might be the final bit of hope in their hopeless world. We have invitations to their homes, to their stages, to their film sets, and to their prisons.

SEEING THE FUTURE

When God speaks to you, whether it be through another human being, a material sign like a billboard or a movie, or directly face to face, it is as if a key unlocks the treasures of your heart that were already there before you were born. Therefore, when God reveals the secret (the word *secret* means Kruptos—a place where treasure is kept) of your heart, the first instinct is to worship God, or to at least feel grateful to Him. Once the treasure of your heart is unlocked, you see yourself as God sees you. This gives you the power to capture the future.

Some people will despise you when you behave in a fashion that displays your predestined occupation. In fact, something I have noted is that any person who hears God is actually delivered from time, and they refuse to allow their "present" to dictate their vision and the progressive truth working in their lives. When you capture the "future," you bring it into your present state of existence, and from that point forward, you are "nourished" by the future instead of being battered by the past or present.

Daniel, a Jewish prophet who was exiled in Babylon (present day Iraq), was able to survive all kinds of things, including being thrown among lions, because he had seen so far into the future that eternal life was controlling his body. He was nourished by the future, a future where his name, his prophecies, and his presence existed. Do you know that you are in the future? You're there only by what you do today. You are making your own personal history, good or bad, by the way you act today, and the only way that you can make good history is by living according to the destiny you were called to by God and God only.

When Jesus was on the cross, there was no nourishment in the hatred and filth surrounding Him; He was being nourished by the future. Christ actually endured the Cross, one of the cruelest deaths, by seeing the joy that was ahead of him (see Heb. 12:2). He saw the future that He was creating because of a sacrifice for humankind.

You and I can endure anything once we catch a glimpse of our future and act accordingly. When you know who you are in the eyes of God, there is an attraction toward you. People will be drawn to you because they are drawn to the light inside of you. You don't always have to make things happen; sometimes you just have to let things happen. The Law of Attraction will draw people to you. The Law of Attraction is the light of tomorrow—God.

ENDNOTES

1. "'Airlines Terror Plot' Disrupted," *BBC News*, 10 August 2006, http://news.bbc.co.uk/2/hi/uk_news/4778575.stm.

2. *Ibid.*

3. "Details Emerge on Alleged Plot to Bomb Airliners," *MSNBC*, 10 August 2006, http://www.msnbc.msn.com/id/14278216/

Chapter 4

A Walk With the Legends

THE prophet is no new phenomenon; history has a long list of controversial representatives who have been called crazy for their outrageous predictions and unusual methods, along with those who actually were crazy. To properly understand the role of the prophet in the modern world and the potential significance of the message, it is essential to take a look down the long historical road from which they have emerged as voices to their world, often becoming martyrs in the process. Ronald Reagan said, "History is a ribbon, always unfurling. History is a journey. As we continue our journey, we think of those who traveled before us and we see and hear again the echoes of our past"[1]

The prophet is one of the most controversial and misunderstood figures of all time. History distinguishes many of those whom God gifted and set apart to hear and speak on His behalf, as well as the preying wolves who arose at various times exploiting and robbing the people of self-respect and simple faith in God. Unfortunately, many of the great prophets we read about today and celebrate as being true voices were grossly misunderstood and suffered persecution for such in their generation. It has been said

CALL ME CRAZY, BUT I'M HEARING GOD

that all things of great value are eventually counterfeited and misrepresented, and the prophet is no exception.

The message of today's prophet is no longer the pointed finger of condemnation, but the extended hand of hope; and an entire generation is recognizing this like never before, and reaching out for it. The object of this book is not necessarily to present the need for prophets today, as much as it is to emphasize the opportunity you have to hear God's voice personally and the benefits that come from following Him. However, the lives of historical and modern prophets reveal much about the art of prophecy and can provide a source of inspiration for you on your journey to discover His voice.

SAINT THOMAS AQUINAS— THE MINISTRY OF THE PROPHET

Saint Thomas Aquinas was an Italian Catholic priest in the Dominican Order and a philosopher who is considered by many Catholics to be the Church's greatest theologian.

St. Thomas is also held in the Roman Catholic Church to be the model teacher for those studying for the priesthood. On the subject of prophecy, St Thomas wrote:

> As the term (Prophecy) is used in mystical theology, it applies both to the prophecies of canonical Scripture and to private prophecies. Understood in its strict sense, it means the foreknowledge of future events, though it may sometimes apply to past events of which there is no memory, and to present hidden things which cannot be known

by the natural light of reason. St. Paul, speaking of prophecy in 1 Corinthians 14, does not confine its meaning to
predictions of future events, but includes under it Divine
inspirations concerning what is secret, whether future or
not. As, however, the manifestation of hidden present mysteries or past events comes under revelation, we have here
to understand by prophecy what is in its strict and proper
sense, namely the revelation of future events. Prophecy
consists in knowledge and in the manifestation of what is
known. The knowledge must be supernatural and infused
by God because it concerns things beyond the natural
power of created intelligence; and the knowledge must be
manifested either by words or signs, because the gift of
prophecy is given primarily for the good of others, and
hence needs to be manifested. It is a Divine light by which
God reveals things concerning the unknown future and by
which these things are in some way represented to the
mind of the prophet, whose duty it is to manifest them to
others.[2]

Despite the fact that charlatans arose at various times, we are
presented over and over again with the positive influence of
prophets upon the history of nations and the benefit of their
divine secrets. The prophet is a chosen instrument who hears from
God through various levels of communication and is chosen to
speak as His representative. His words are not his own but are
given from a Higher Source and are meant to bring hope and
enrichment to the individual and community. The words of
prophets have impacted lives insomuch that they have changed
the course of history, which hinges on the response of the recipi-
ents. Though there are too many historical examples of valuable

prophetic voices that have emerged over the centuries to list them all here, there are some valuable insights that can be gained about the office by examining some of their lives a bit closer.

As Winston Churchill said, "Every prophet has to come from civilization, but every prophet has to go into the wilderness. He must have a strong impression of a complex variety and all that it has to give and he must serve a period of isolation and meditation. That is the process by which psychic dynamite is made."[3]

The first man, Adam, is considered the first prophet of God according to both Judaism and Islam. The Book of Genesis tells us that Adam communed with God as a friend, but because of the lack of detail provided in the Torah regarding the prophetic aspect of his life, most teachers and scholars of the Christian faith maintain a neutral position or find the matter of little relevance.

ABRAHAM— ## PROPHET TO THREE RELIGIONS

Abraham is the first prophet named in the ancient manuscripts of the Torah, and his life illuminates a predetermined design for all who would follow in his footsteps. All true prophets, like Abraham, were first and foremost friends of God (see Gen. 20:7). It was only from this place of cultivated friendship that a prophet was trusted to speak on behalf of the Almighty.

According to the Torah, Abraham was born in the city of Ur in Southern Mesopotamia, present-day Iraq, and fathered two sons, Ishmael and Isaac. This has remained the center of a controversial, ongoing religious debate among the Jews and Muslims. Perhaps seeming completely out of his mind to his friends and family,

Abraham took a risk and followed the voice of his Friend on a great journey to find the new land that was promised to him and his descendants to become a great nation of their own.

Abraham journeyed from Mesopotamia to the land of Canaan, around 2,000 b.c. Because of his obedience, Abraham was granted the honorable title "Father of many nations." Through all, God positioned Abraham to become what He had promised to make him—a blessing to all of the peoples on the earth (see Gen. 12:2-3), expressing God's original intention and purpose for the prophet. This design can be recognized not only in Abraham, but also through the lives of many who followed faithfully in the calling of prophet throughout the ages.

Of course, when talking about prophets, some may conjure images of the angry, old, white-haired figure, pointing a long bony finger while screaming fiery predictions of great judgments upon the earth, as depicted in some movies. Although there are times when God has used the prophet to deliver such dramatic words and guide the people through the events that followed, these were the result of man's defiant departure from the voice of his Creator and God's strategic action to prevent further decadence and loss. Even in the times of pronounced judgments, the people were promised the return of God's blessing, if they would turn back to Him.

Moses—
Greatest of All Prophets

The life of Moses reveals much about the chaos surrounding the phenomenon of the prophet and gives further insight regarding his purpose as one of the first messengers who was initially rejected by the people to whom he was sent. Moses is considered by many to be the greatest prophet to ever walk the earth, holding a degree of authority unequalled until the coming of Jesus Christ.

> *And there arose no more a prophet in Israel like unto Moses, whom the Lord knew face to face, in all the signs and wonders, which he sent by him, to do in the land of Egypt to Pharaoh, and to all his servants, and to his whole land, and all the mighty hand, and great miracles, which Moses did before all Israel* (Deuteronomy 34:10-12 KJV).

There were other prophets with Moses, but only of a lesser rank, such as Aaron and Maria, Eldad and Medad, to whom God spoke to in dreams and visions. The highest level of communication was reserved for His friend Moses, who was most faithful in all His house (see Num. 12:7). Moses is given a place of great honor in most major religions, including Christianity, Judaism, and Islam.

According to orthodox Jews, he is considered the "Father of all Prophets." History celebrates Moses as a Hebrew religious leader, military leader, historian, and prophet who lived according to the Hebrew calendar, between the 7th of Adar 2368 and 7th of Adar 2488. The Torah, the first five books of the Bible, is also considered by most scholars to be the work of Moses.

Though the prophet was intended to be a blessing to the nations, Moses was chosen to represent God in a confrontation with the Pharaoh of Egypt to extricate the Hebrew people. This was perhaps the most dramatic assignment for the office of the prophet in all of history, demonstrating the sovereignty of God in world affairs. Moses exercised divine authority through signs and wonders, even over the weather and the natural elements, as he led the Hebrews out from under the heavy oppression and slavery executed by the Egyptian rulers.

According to the ancient Hebrew manuscripts, Moses was born to a Hebrew mother who hid him when Pharaoh ordered all newborn Hebrew boys of his time to be killed. He was soon found and adopted into the Egyptian royal family. Years later, after killing an Egyptian slave master, he fled and became a shepherd, where he remained until the time of his famous experience of hearing God speak to him from the burning bush. Moses was called to action and sent to confront a powerful world leader, the Pharaoh of Egypt, and demand the freedom of the Hebrew people, the Israelites.

The role of the prophet would now bring the demonstration of the supernatural through a series of public dealings with Pharaoh by God as he corrected the decades-long injustice. Astounding displays of unparalleled signs and wonders were performed at the words of Moses, shaking Egypt to its very core. Egypt was consumed by plague after plague right before the eyes of both the Hebrews and the Egyptians, until Pharaoh reluctantly agreed to release them.

All of this brought a new perspective to the vital role of the prophet and the reality of God's interest in world affairs. Though some refused to believe Moses when he first came on the scene, undoubtedly many experienced a newfound faith in the God of the Hebrews through these supernatural acts; and despite the initial assumed madness, a healthy respect was gained for His chosen voice.

The ancient manuscripts tell us that through this great journey, Moses and the liberated Hebrew people encountered many other instances of God's supernatural intervention for their provision and protection in their search for the Promised Land. Moses' role as prophet became much more than just delivering the message to Pharaoh and leading a mass exodus from Egypt.

In the rapidly developing Israelite community, Moses sat as judge to offer guidance and spiritual counsel in various civil disputes and in countless matters for which the people sought the will of God. After seeing the overwhelming workload and stress Moses was under, his father-in-law, Jethro, advised him to specially select and appoint a group of judges to serve under his leadership, so that he could focus on weightier matters, including prayer and hearing God for the nation. Moses concurred and appointed those who would serve in this new office as judges of Israel.

God's Desire To Speak Directly

In Exodus chapter 19, God told Moses to gather the people because He wanted to speak directly to them Himself. After the people gathered around the mountain and experienced the intense sounds of thunder and vivid visual expressions of smoke and lightning from the descent of the Almighty to meet Moses, they begged their leader to keep God from ever speaking to them again personally, and to assume the duty of conversing on their behalf.

At the mountain, Moses was given the Ten Commandments to present to the young, wavering nation, demanding a return to the core values that were lost, in part, during the years of influence under Egyptian bondage. The law was received; however, the splendor of hearing God's voice was tragically abandoned to be discovered and cultivated primarily through those whom many would call crazy—the prophets. As Socrates wrote, "I decided that it was not wisdom that enabled [poets] to write their poetry, but a kind of instinct or inspiration, such as you find in seers and prophets who deliver all their sublime messages without knowing in the least what they mean."[4]

The Prophet Is Only Human

Since the fear of making a mistake or being wrong is one of the greatest weapons the enemy will use against you to prevent you from hearing God's voice in your own life and for your own world, I want to deal with a misunderstanding regarding false prophets that has incited fear in many regarding the subject.

Although I do not believe it's important to defend my reputation as a prophet of Christ, I do believe it's very important to have an accurate biblical foundation and a historical perspective regarding the subject from which to derive principles and provide a reliable source of knowledge. This has always been essential, especially for those called to this office, to avoid the possibility of being deceived by erroneous teachings or even becoming counter productive to the call through immaturity and ignorance.

Even in the early stages of Christ's ministry, He warned His followers in the writings of several gospel accounts, including Matthew's, to beware of false prophets, who are in sheep's clothing, but inwardly they are ravenous wolves (see Matt. 7:15). Being fore-warned by the greatest of all prophets, who accurately foresaw the impostors who have come and gone since then, manipulating and deceiving the people, and those yet to emerge, should cause us to not take the matter lightly.

Christ's words show that a false prophet is one who portrays to be something he's not. Though he seems to be one of the sheep, on careful inspection it can be seen that he is actually an extremely hungry predator lurking upon his prey. That's why it is important to judge the fruit of the tree to determine if it is good or bad. On the other hand, many today are restricted so much by an unhealthy fear they would rather dismiss the idea of prophets in today's world, and the possibility of hearing God's voice for themselves altogether than to take a risk in pursuit of this lost treasure and benefit from His intended purpose of interacting in our lives.

Because there were numerous prophets in a given generation during the time of the Exodus, the matter arose of who should be trusted and believed to speak on behalf of the Almighty. We find in the ancient manuscripts many examples of prophets and dreamers, functioning on various levels of authority and relating uniquely in their community and societies.

It's also clear that the prophets functioned in various levels of prominence and national influence, depending on the specific gifting and assignment each was given. These different levels can be seen in the example given of Eldad and Medad, who prophesied within the Israelite camp, as reported by Joshua to Moses. Though Joshua told Moses to stop them, Moses answered in Numbers chapter 11,

Joshua, son of Nun, who had been Moses' aide since youth, spoke up and said, "Moses, my lord, stop them!" But

Moses replied, "Are you jealous for my sake? I wish that all the Lord's people were prophets and that the Lord would put His Spirit on them" (Numbers 11:28-29).

This surprising answer from Moses showed again the original intention God had for humankind to hear His voice for themselves, and conveyed the desire of the mature prophet to see others excel in the field in which he was called to provide inspiration.

As the immature dreamers and prophets began to share and discuss their revelations in the communities, the frauds also arose, lying about dreams and visions, making up prophecies, and stealing the words of other prophets as they attempted to exploit the people and selfishly promote themselves to a greater place of prominence.

To compound the problem even further, there also arose prophets speaking on behalf of false gods, confusing the people and causing them to turn away from the simple faith that was taught and received from their forefathers, Abraham, Isaac, Jacob, and their ordained leader, Moses. With this becoming an increasing problem, the Book of Deuteronomy reveals some general laws that Moses put into place and strictly enforced to discourage the agenda of the impostors and deceivers.

JUDGING PROPHECY

This brings us to the myth that has stopped many dead in their tracks who desire to hear God speak to them. It is frequently misquoted or taken out of context from the Book of Deuteronomy, chapters 13 and 18. From Moses' instructions we will look at two basic scenarios regarding the ancient prophets and their predictions. First we will look at those prophets whose words do come to pass (see Deut. 13), and then second those whose words do not come to pass (see Deut. 18).

Many within the modern establishment of the church, who oppose my work and that of other forefront prophetic voices, adhere to an ideal that demands nothing less than 100 percent fulfillment of a prophet's words and predictions, otherwise condemning one as a false prophet. I do realize that there are some well-meaning individuals who may sincerely misunderstand the subject, perhaps from following the opinions of other respected leaders.

However, I have found that many who believe and teach this variation usually despise anything that does not fit into their narrow-minded view of God and become quite inflamed when challenged by its accurate quotation, as well as examples of biblical prophets who did not measure up to their demanded standard.

To help overcome this obstacle in your own journey to hear God, we'll take a closer look at the ancient manuscript to precisely extract the truth found on this subject. This is the message that Moses had given in this composition of the Torah.

If there arises among you a prophet or a dreamer of dreams, and he gives you a sign or a wonder, and the sign or the wonder comes to pass, of which he spoke to you, saying, "Let us go after other gods"—which you have not known— "and let us serve them," you shall not listen to the words of that prophet or that dreamer of dreams, for the Lord your God is testing you to know whether you love the Lord your

God with all your heart and with all your soul. You shall walk after the Lord your God and fear Him, and keep His commandments and obey His voice; you shall serve Him and hold fast to Him. But that prophet or that dreamer of dreams shall be put to death, because he has spoken in order to turn you away from the Lord your God... (Deuteronomy 13:1-5).

In this first scenario we find the prophet or dreamer of dreams whose words *did* in fact come to pass and attempted to exploit the audience and lead them astray to serve false gods. It's clear, according to the Mosaic Law, that he was to be stoned.

Stoning was used, not only during Moses' times, but also later throughout history in a number of places as a form of capital punishment. The practice became common in Judaism, among the ancient Greeks, and later in Islam, where stoning was promoted in their religious texts as the punishment for a variety of offenses. Some crimes that warranted stoning included blasphemy, prostitution, adultery, murder, and apostasy. Although many have suffered martyrdom from the abused law of stoning, including those who followed Christ, His teachings discourage this practice.

In Judaism, strategically, there was no appointed person to execute a criminal because that person would be responsible and guilty of murder. In fact, those who were witnesses of the event were required to throw the first stones, serving the community as a societal punishment to the criminal and preventing any definite way of tracking the individual whose stone killed the condemned. This would protect all who participated in the act since no one specifically could be held responsible.

Although not common, it is reported that stoning remains as a form of execution in several Islamic countries where the religion dictates the law and people can be punished or killed for minor violations.

To put the instruction by Moses for condemning and stoning prophets in its correct context, it's important to review the entire 13th chapter of Deuteronomy, which deals with instructing the people to stone anyone who attempts to turn the people away from the Lord, including brothers, sisters, sons, daughters, or even a spouse.

> *If your brother, the son of your mother, your son or your daughter, the wife of your bosom, or your friend who is as your own soul, secretly entices you, saying, "Let us go and serve other gods," which you have not known, neither you nor your fathers, of the gods of the people which are all around you, near to you or far off from you, from one end of the earth to the other end of the earth, you shall not consent to him or listen to him, nor shall your eye pity him, nor shall you spare him or conceal him; but you shall surely kill him; your hand shall be first against him to put him to death, and afterward the hand of all the people. And you shall stone him with stones until he dies, because he sought to entice you away from the Lord your God, who brought you out of the land of Egypt, from the house of bondage. So all Israel shall hear and fear, and not again do such wickedness as this among you* (Deuteronomy 13:6-11).

In these verses of Scripture, the people were instructed to stone everyone guilty of this grievous offense, not just prophets.

However, since the prophetic office carries with it a great stigma that arouses various reactions, especially among the religious, many find it easier to focus on the potential failure of a prophet than that of the average person. Though stoning is not permitted in most cultures today, those who despise the prophets usually find their satisfaction in other crafty attempts to arouse fears, suspicion, and unreasonable judgments.

Hundreds of years after the Law was given, the teachings and life of the Prophet Jesus Christ radically challenged the established religious community in many ways, even regarding the subject of stoning. Christ taught that the law of stoning resulted in the death of many of God's choice messengers, signifying a gross abuse of its original purpose, since the time of its initiation.

> *O Jerusalem, Jerusalem, the one who kills the prophets and stones those who are sent to her! How often I wanted to gather your children together, as a hen gathers her chicks under her wings, but you were not willing* (Matthew 23:37).

This was clearly an attempt of the corrupt religious system to silence God's voice in the earth in the generations following Moses and it has continued its work even to this day. When confronted by the religious leaders of the day who wanted to test Him regarding their desire to stone a woman exposed and taken in the act of adultery, Christ demonstrated mercy inconceivable to their narrow-minded view of God. Though they tested Christ, when about to stone a woman taken in adultery, His words disarmed each of her accusers.

In John 8:1-12, they said *"Moses, in the law, commanded us that such should be stoned. But what do You say?" This they said, testing Him, that they might have something of which to accuse Him."* However, his simple reply was, *"He who is without sin among you, let him throw a stone at her first." At this they all walked away, and Christ said, "neither do I condemn you; go and sin no more."*

This simple display of God's love and forgiveness through the Prophet Jesus Christ, spared the life of a woman who was to be stoned, and signified the beginning of a new era in which God would deal with people by His Spirit, rather than strictly according to laws. This newly demonstrated grace was a symbol of the life of this Prophet, foreseen by Moses, who would eventually lay His own life down for the spiritual freedom of all people. It also provided a new example for those who would become His disciples and prophets and for the radical positive message that they would spread throughout the world.

WHEN THE PROPHET'S WORDS DO NOT COME TO PASS

The second scenario is one when the prophet's words did not come to pass. Contradicting the abuses of the religious system of many generations, including some of the modern world, Moses instructed that a prophet whose words do not come to pass was not to be feared. However, Deuteronomy chapter 18 also gives further instruction regarding how to judge whether or not a word is given by God and how to respond to the prophet whose predictions did *not* come to pass. It begins with Moses' prophecy about the Prophet that would eventually arise and be like him and the importance of His message, which is widely accepted in the Christian community as that of Jesus Christ.

The Lord your God will raise up for you a Prophet like me from your midst, from your brethren. Him you shall hear, according to all you desired of the Lord your God in Horeb in the day of the assembly, saying, "Let me not hear again the voice of the Lord my God, nor let me see this great fire anymore, lest I die."

"And the Lord said to me: 'What they have spoken is good. I will raise up for them a Prophet like you from among their brethren, and will put My words in His mouth, and He shall speak to them all that I command Him. And it shall be that whoever will not hear My words, which He speaks in My name, I will require it of him. But the prophet who presumes to speak a word in My name, which I have not commanded him to speak, or who speaks in the name of other gods, that prophet shall die." And if you say in your heart, "How shall we know the word which the Lord has not spoken?"— when a prophet speaks in the name of the Lord, if the thing does not happen or come to pass, that is the thing which the Lord has not spoken; the prophet has spoken it presumptuously; you shall not be afraid of him (Deuteronomy 18:15-22).

In other words, if the message is really from God, it will come to pass. If the message is not from God, it will not come to pass. This was the test for whether or not a word or dream was from God. There was no need in stoning a prophet if his words did not come to pass since his words carried no weight of credibility.

Since Moses could not possibly go among the people to judge every word or dream that was being shared, he simply educated them regarding how to judge the prophecies that were being given in the community. Although this may seem insignificant, it was critical to help them properly discern which words possibly were and which were not of divine origin.

People feared the true prophet in those days, having witnessed firsthand the unearthly authority demonstrated by Moses, even inflicting dreadful judgments on the Egyptians, and this warranted a genuine basis for fear of the prophet. Therefore, Moses instructed the people to no longer be afraid of those whose predictions did not come to pass. This is the opposite approach of many religious zealots, even today, who spread panic and have made it their life's work to look for inaccuracies and flaws in others. According to Deuteronomy chapter 13, those who believe that the sign of a true prophet is simply accuracy or that his words always come to pass, are actually in greater danger of deception.

On the other hand, it is important now to clarify that this Law did not say to stone the presumed messenger for giving a failed prediction, but specified rather that the prophet who spoke presumptuously or in the name of other gods shall die. This warning is the same warning given to Adam in the Garden, regarding the tree of knowledge of good and evil. In the Book of Genesis 2:16-17 it is written: *"And the Lord God commanded the man, saying, 'Of every tree of the garden you may freely eat; but of the tree of the knowledge of good and evil you shall not eat, for in the day that you eat of it you shall surely die.'"*

As the story goes, Adam and his wife, Eve, eventually ate from the tree that they were clearly warned not to eat from and yet were not put to death by God for doing so, as it would be easy to assume in reading. Adam and Eve were not killed for their outright disobedience. In fact, after they had tasted the forbidden fruit and

God pronounced the curse that would come upon the human race as a result, the ancient manuscripts tell us that God made coats of skins for them to cover their shame and nakedness. Even though they messed things up, God did not kill Adam and Eve or disown them. In fact, they went on to have children and lived a long time. According to the genealogies of Genesis, Adam died at the ripe old age of 930.

So what was the point in saying that the presumptuous prophet and the prophet of false gods whose words did not come to pass, would die? These who never really knew the voice of the true God or may have once known and forfeited their right to it, were without true prophetic vision. They could not operate from an eternal perspective of divine authority, being limited to their mere natural vision to guide them. Proverbs 29:18 says, "*Where there is no vision, the people perish.*"

In conclusion, the heart of the matter was to equip the people, at least at a basic level, to recognize God's voice for themselves and to protect them from the impostors and corrupting influence of false religions. However, the Law was not perfect. The writings do not provide a clear definition of what a false prophet was but did educate the people to no longer fear those whose predictions failed. It was apparently effective for some time, bringing order and accountability to those who claimed to represent God as they spoke. However, the coming decades and centuries would yield some complicated instances of prophets giving predictions that could not be judged precisely using these basic instructions.

After the time of Moses, many other true prophetic voices continued to emerge and be used to speak on behalf of the Almighty. Though controversial, there are examples even in the ancient manuscripts, the Bible, perhaps overlooked by the casual reader, which show that things did not always come to pass as they were predicted by some of the most well-known prophetic voices. To understand the dynamics of these prophetic predictions properly, you must understand that God's actions are not always His original intentions.

INTENTIONS VERSUS ACTIONS

When God speaks to human beings about their future, His word is based on His intention to see all people blessed. He will make known His intentions without a doubt in His mind that He will *do it*. However, His *actions* are many times determined by the response of the recipient. It is then left to that person to decide whether to accept or reject God's intention for their lives. This is hard for many people to understand, but God's actions do not always line up with His intentions because He has given us the power to decide our own destiny.

People make mistakes every day of their lives, and unfortunately, this often determines the outcome of a word given. God is *all powerful*, but He has given us a will to choose for ourselves and has always patiently allowed us to do so. God's *intention* was for Moses to bring water from the rock by "speaking" to it instead of hitting it: God's *actions* were determined by Moses' anger toward the people and his disobedience to God. God's *intention* was that the people of Israel would hear His voice directly. His *actions* were determined by the people's fear of His voice and their request to never hear Him speak to them directly; instead they appointed Moses to go and hear for them and to tell them what God was saying.

God's *intention* was for Samson to be the strong man who would rise up against the Philistines with a healthy body and mind; His *actions* were determined by Samson's will to reveal his secret strength under the seduction of Delilah, thereby fulfilling God's will with no eyes and in chains. God's *intention* was that Eli and his family would carry the priesthood throughout their generations; His *actions* were determined by Eli's toleration of sin in the temple, and God said: "I did say that…but now I say…."

God's *intention* was that Israel would remain free from the enemy's control during the time of Gideon. A prophet gave them the reason why they were overpowered and controlled by the Midianites. His *actions* were determined by Israel's disobedience and sin. God's *intention* was for Moses to take the children of Israel into the Promised Land; ten spies came with a bad report and influenced the wills of over 3.5 million people. God's *action* was to force them to walk in circles for 40 years and then give it to them. God's *actions* were determined by man's unbelief and their desire to go back to Egypt.

THE JUDGES—
PROPHETS IN A TIME OF TRANSITION

In the time of the judges, there arose Deborah (see Judg. 4-5), who was called "a mother in Israel." She served as a judge among the people and communicated God's orders concerning the War of Independence to Barak and the tribes. The word of God was rare in those days of anarchy as He dealt with the wavering nation by letting them go astray unto their own demise. Over this period, there were 15 judges in all, the last being Samuel, whose divine mission was to restore the code of the elder and to oversee the beginning of the royalty of Israel.

SAMUEL—
PROPHET TO THE KINGS

Samuel, according to rabbinical literature, was the last of the Hebrew judges and the first of the major prophets who began to prophesy throughout the land of Israel. According to First Samuel 1:20, Hannah was the mother of Samuel; and she named him in memory of her answered prayer request to God for a child. Samuel was the only prophet of whom it is said that God, *"let none of his words fall to the ground"* (1 Sam. 3:19). Samuel was used to identify and anoint the very first King of Israel, Saul, as well as his successor, David.

Under the guidance of Samuel, or at least closely united to him, we find for the first time the prophets (see 1 Sam. 10:5), grouped together with the accompaniment of musical instruments. It seems these prophets used music for worship, to set the tone from which to release their revelations, and possibly to inspire their followers to make united declarations. Although not much detail is given regarding these prophets, it's possible they joined Samuel playing music and speaking as oracles under his leadership among the people. They displayed some giftings similar to those that were later bestowed upon Christ's disciples, as recorded in the Book of Acts.

The prophet King David was also a skilled musician and warrior. Using the sword and the harp, he demonstrated his kingship and defeated his enemies. However, it wasn't the harp, lyre, or sword that made him a great King, it was his heart. As a musician, my style of prophetic delivery is also strongly connected to music, and with it I create a prophetic atmosphere to prepare the people for a moment with God.

Isaiah—
Statesman Prophet

The prophet Isaiah accurately predicted many things, including the virgin birth of Christ (see Isa. 7:14). Isaiah was a great prophetic voice who, according to historical writings, suffered a horrible death by being sawn in two. Isaiah also gave a prediction that would be difficult to judge by simply by the law. Prophetically he announced to the dying King Hezekiah that he should immediately put his house in order because he would in fact die. Hezekiah wept and immediately prayed and reminded God of all the good he had done in his lifetime.

Hezekiah's response to the prophetic prediction changed God's mind, and he was immediately granted another 15 years to live, but Isaiah's initial prediction did not come to pass. This is a situation where you can see that the Law was not enough to judge every prediction properly. According to the standard some hold today, Isaiah would have been called a false prophet because his initial prediction did not come to pass. However, this example demonstrates the unfolding progression of prophecy which is determined by the response of the recipient.

In those days Hezekiah was sick and near death. And Isaiah the prophet, the son of Amoz, went to him and said to him, "*Thus says the Lord: 'Set your house in order, for you shall die, and not live.'*" *Then he turned his face toward the wall, and prayed to the Lord, saying, "Remember now, O Lord, I pray, how I have walked before You in truth and with a loyal heart, and have done what was good in Your sight." And Hezekiah wept bitterly.*

And it happened, before Isaiah had gone out into the middle court, that the word of the Lord came to him, saying, "Return and tell Hezekiah the leader of My people, 'Thus says the Lord, the God of David your father: "I have heard your prayer, I have seen your tears; surely I will heal you. On the third day you shall go up to the house of the Lord. And I will add to your days fifteen years. I will deliver you and this city from the hand of the king of Assyria; and I will defend this city for My own sake, and for the sake of My servant David."'" (2 Kings 20:1-6).

JONAH—
RELUCTANT PROPHET

God told the prophet Jonah to go and prophesy to the city of Nineveh that it would be destroyed. Jonah, being apprehensive, first fled from Nineveh, because he didn't want to do it, knowing that God may change His mind and not destroy them. Yet, the story says that God put Jonah through some very tough circumstances until he would finally agree to go and prophesy. After Jonah went to the city Nineveh and pronounced the destruction would come in 40 days, the people responded just as God desired.

Their repentance changed God's mind, and He did not destroy a single person:

> *Now the word of the Lord came to Jonah the second time, saying, "Arise, go to Nineveh, that great city, and preach to it the message that I tell you." So Jonah arose and went to Nineveh, according to the word of the Lord. Now Nineveh was an exceedingly great city, a three-day journey in extent. And Jonah began to enter the city on the first day's walk. Then he cried out and said, "Yet forty days, and Nineveh shall be overthrown!"*

> *So the people of Nineveh believed God, proclaimed a fast, and put on sackcloth, from the greatest to the least of them. Then word came to the king of Nineveh; and he arose from his throne and laid aside his robe, covered himself with sackcloth and sat in ashes. And he caused it to be proclaimed and published throughout Nineveh by the decree of the king and his nobles, saying, Let neither man nor beast, herd nor flock, taste anything; do not let them eat, or drink water. But let man and beast be covered with sackcloth, and cry mightily to God; yes, let every one turn from his evil way and from the violence that is in his hands. Who can tell if God will turn and relent, and turn away from His fierce anger, so that we may not perish? Then God saw their works, that they turned from their evil way; and God relented from the disaster that He had said He would bring upon them, and He did not do it* (Jonah 3:1-10).

To the average skeptic of the day, Jonah probably appeared to be completely out of his mind, especially when his prediction did not come to pass. He did not give the stipulation in his prediction that if they repented God would prevent the destruction of the city; nonetheless, it was used in such as way that it motivated the people to get back to where they were supposed to be.

According to the Law, it may be said that his word was not from God, since it did not come to pass. It seemed there was no threat of Jonah being stoned, but he very well may have lost his credibility with some, while others must have celebrated him as a hero for helping them prevent the predicted disaster.

What I am saying is, God has given you the gift of free will and for you to see His revealed intention for your life come to pass, you must remain in agreement with it and take the appropriate actions.

Your response to God determines whether or not you will enter the promise He gave you. You have been given the right to determine whether or not His intention for your life will come to pass. You are responsible for your future, and there is nothing anyone can say that will change it, especially if you are determined to walk another course in life. God leaves the matter in your hands, and He then responds accordingly. This makes your image and idea of God a critical factor in the process, so you have the utmost confidence that He truly wants the best for you.

As one maturing in any gift or vocation, there will also be times when you will be wrong about what you believe God showed you. This is when it's important to have the proper basis to judge what you think may be a potential word from God. If it opposes the revealed and established truth about the ways and character of God, then you do not need to waste your time searching out the matter. Even when you feel you have weighed the word carefully, there will be times when what you felt God may have shown you is proven incorrect. Don't let that discourage you on your journey.

There are times when some of my predictions have not come to pass and appear to be wrong, and for this I can only judge myself. However, it's a tragic misunderstanding to believe that God will only speak to us when we are perfect and that a prophet cannot make any mistakes. That's not only ludicrous; it's inconsistent with the nature of God revealed in the teachings and examples of the greatest leaders of the faith, found in both the Hebrew and Greek Scriptures.

I believe that a person who is said to be a prophet should have a track record of accuracy backing their words, but perfection is not required to be a voice for God. The Source is complete, but the voice that is chosen to communicate the word is merely human. It's God in us, expressing Himself as a friend to humankind. This prophetic amalgamation is the beauty of being an instrument of God.

Simply being inaccurate in any vocation, skill, gift, or calling doesn't make one false. A teacher may unintentionally give some wrong or misleading information, but that alone doesn't make the teacher false. The same goes for prophets. The human characteristics of a prophet are independent of the message God has given and they do not negate the validity of the prophecy. The important thing to remember is that God is never wrong and that everyone must acknowledge their own imperfections before Him.

Because I know this is true, I will never stop prophesying, for I know this is what God has called me to do, though I will always remain accountable to my friends and counselors. I will always endeavor to obey God as best I can, for my desire is to reach out to people from a heart of love and compassion. It's also important that you do not allow the fear of being wrong to stop you. The reward far outweighs the potential risks, if you will follow His voice. As George Mueller said, "The beginning of anxiety is the end of faith, and the beginning of true faith is the end of anxiety."[5]

ELIJAH AND ELISHA— PROPHETS IN TIMES OF CRISIS

The two greatest figures of prophecy between the times of Samuel and Isaiah were Elijah and Elisha. Israel was corrupted by the worship of false gods, especially by Jezebel, the wife of Ahab, who had introduced the worship of her Phoenician gods. Israel's faith was also divided between the worship of their God and that of the false god, Baal.

At that time, Elijah came on the scene, and with preaching and miracles, he led Israel back to the true God. This impacted the people and lessened the influence of the gods of Canaan. Then at Carmel, Elijah demonstrated divine power over the prophets of Baal in a dramatic confrontation. Eventually, he disappeared in a fiery chariot, leaving the mantle and a double portion of his spirit to his disciple, Elisha.

Elisha successfully carried on the work begun by Elijah against the Canaanite idolatry and became such an asset to the Kingdom that King Joash wept for his death and said, *"My father! My father! The chariots of Israel and their horsemen!"* (2 Kings 13:14). Both of these men demonstrated the supernatural ministry of the prophet, and more detailed accounts of their lives can be found in the

Books of First and Second Kings. They are also mentioned by Christ in the gospels.

PROPHETS AFTER CHRIST

Some claim that the role of the prophet ceased when Christ finished His work and when the dispensation of the Church began. But historical writings surrender accounts of the lives of many prophets who have lived since Christ's earthly ministry, including those of the New Testament: Agabus, Barnabus, Judas, Silas, John, and Paul. Agabus was known at the time for accurately predicting a great famine, and he also predicted the arrest of the apostle Paul in the Book of Acts: "*And as we stayed many days, a certain prophet named Agabus came down from Judea. When he had come to us, he took Paul's belt, bound his own hands and feet, and said, 'Thus says the Holy Spirit, So shall the Jews at Jerusalem bind the man who owns this belt, and deliver him into the hands of the Gentiles'*" (Acts 21:10-11).

Agabus was a prophet of Christ, and the foresight that he was given helped Paul prepare for what he would have to face. The Book of Acts, which is included in the canonization of the New Testament Scriptures, is a historical record of the Acts of the Apostles that followed Christ after His death and includes examples of others who experienced the voice of God.

In the early days of the Church, supernatural expressions of divine power became known as the gifts of the Spirit. Prophecy was not only demonstrated by the new movement's spiritual leaders but was also taught to be a gift for the benefit of all and available to everyone who would believe.

About the middle of the second century, Montanus appeared as a new prophet in Phrygia. Under him also the prophetesses Priscilla and Maximilla appeared. Prophecy was, indeed, the most prominent feature of the new movement. In the third century we discover a young prophetess, Perpetua, who died a martyr's death because of her commitment to Christ.

The Didache was an early church manual written in the late first or early second century. In the Didache we discover various references to the prophet. It gives insight into how Christians during that period of time still respected the work of the prophet.

Throughout history there have been many prophets, and some of these, such as Nostradamus who lived during the 16th century, have made interesting predictions concerning world events. He gave his prophecies in the form of verses known as quatrains, and they demand intense scrutiny, examination, and interpretation. Many believe that Nostradamus predicted the deaths of popes, world wars, and even the attacks on the World Trade Center on 9-11-2001. However, because many of the quatrains are very ambiguous, it is not certain that people's interpretations of his prophecies are accurate, and it is impossible to verify the truth of the prophecies themselves.

In 1917, three shepherd children near Fatima, Portugal, experienced "an apparition of the Virgin Mary." It is said that the mother of Jesus gave them three "secrets" for the Body of Christ. These are known as the Fatima prophecies.

The Roman Catholic Church believes that the Holy Spirit inspired these prophecies. In the first secret, the children were shown a vision of hell. The second secret told about the rise of Russia and included many interesting details about Russia's role in history. The third secret may well be the most interesting of all, and it was revealed by the Vatican after the attempt in 1981 to assassinate Pope John Paul II.

The following is a significant portion of its message: "The 'bishop clothed in white,' who is the pope, 'makes his way with great effort toward the cross amid the corpses of those who were martyred. He, too, falls to the ground, apparently dead, under a burst of gunfire.'"

Many believe these prophecies serve as warnings from God.

A prophet of Christ is one who speaks on behalf of one God and in His name, and lives according to the teachings of Christ. He or she is chosen not only to speak messages that conform to His teachings, but despite modern misunderstandings, they may also convey the message creatively, through various means including music, poetry, or specifically prompted actions to communicate God's feelings or other details in the message. The prophet should never contradict the teachings of Christ and must present messages that accurately represent the intentions of God for humankind, even though their words may often challenge traditional religious views.

There is no doubt that prophets are needed in our world today. In the middle of a crisis, the prophet sees the contradiction, and inspires others to see it and agree with him for its emergence. He sees beyond today's present crisis, revealing a message of hope from the inspiration of the future. In the middle of pain, he feels joy. In poverty, he celebrates abundance. The prophet's life and message are a constant contradiction to present limitations and are meant to inspire the people to trust in the inevitable, supernatural intervention of God.

THE CATHOLIC CHURCH AND PROPHETS—
THREE TYPES OF PROPHECY

In March 1907, the Catholic Church assembled the first Catholic encyclopedia which was designed to give authoritative information on the entire cycle of Catholic interests, action, and doctrine. The encyclopedia was intended to serve the Roman Catholic Church, documenting all of the Catholic accomplishments and some others in nearly all intellectual and professional pursuits, including artists, educators, poets, and scientists. Each subject was studied and researched carefully.

The Church's official view regarding prophets and prophecy was carefully addressed with wisdom, following centuries of deepened misunderstandings, as they carefully searched the Scriptures and other historical documents.

The following is a helpful explanation of the three kinds of prophecy, as written by St. Thomas Aquinas in his *Summa Theologica*. These are contained in the Catholic Encyclopedia dated 1913.

Writers on mystical theology consider prophecies with reference to the illumination of the mind, to the objects revealed, and to the means by which the knowledge is conveyed to the human mind. By reason of the illumination of the mind prophecy may be either perfect or imperfect. It is called perfect when not only the thing revealed, but the revelation itself, is made known—that is, when the prophet knows that it is God who speaks. The prophecy is imperfect when the recipient does not know clearly or sufficiently from whom the revelation precedes, or whether it is the prophetic or individual spirit that speaks. This is called the prophetic instinct, wherein it is possible that a man may be deceived, as it happened in the case of Nathan who said to David when he was thinking of building the Temple of God: "Go, do all that is in thy heart, because the Lord is with thee" (II Kings, vii, 3). But that very night the Lord commanded the Prophet to return to the king and say that the glory of the building of the temple was reserved, not for him, but for his son. St. Gregory, as quoted by Benedict XIV, explains that some holy prophets, through the frequent practice of prophesying, have of themselves predicted some things, believing that therein they were influenced by the spirit of prophecy.

By reason of the object there are three kinds of prophecy according to St. Thomas (Summa II-II:174:1): prophecy of denunciation, of foreknowledge, and of predestination.

1 – Prophecy of Denunciation

❋ In the first kind God reveals future events according to the order of secondary causes, which may be hindered from taking effect by other causes which would require a miraculous power to prevent, and these may or may not happen, though the prophets do not express it but seem to speak absolutely. Isaias spoke thus when he said to Ezechias: "Take order with thy house, for thou shalt die, and not live" (Is., xxxviii,1). To this kind belongs the prophecy of promise, as that mentioned in 1 Kings, ii,30: "I said indeed that thy house, and the house of thy father should minister in my sight, forever," which was not fulfilled. It was a conditional promise made to Heli which was dependent upon other causes which prevented its fulfilment.

2 – Prophecy of Foreknowledge

✳ The second, that of foreknowledge, takes place when God reveals future events which depend upon created free will and which He sees present from eternity. They have reference to life and death, to wars and dynasties, to the affairs of Church and State, as well as to the affairs of individual life.

3 – Prophecy of Predestination

✳ The third kind, the prophecy of predestination, takes place when God reveals what He alone will do, and what He sees present in eternity and in His absolute decree. This includes not only the secret of predestination to grace and to glory, but also those things which God has absolutely decreed to do by His own supreme power, and which will infallibly come to pass.

The objects of prophecy may also be viewed in respect to human knowledge:

✳ when an event may be beyond the possible natural knowledge of the prophet, but may be within the range of human knowledge and known to others who witness the occurrence, as, for instance, the result of the battle of Lepanto revealed to St. Pius V;

✳ when the object surpasses the knowledge of all men, not that it is unknowable but that the human mind cannot naturally receive the knowledge, such as the mystery of the Holy Trinity, or the mystery of predestination;

＊ when the things that are beyond the power of the human mind to know are not in themselves knowable because their truth is not yet determined, such as future contingent things which depend upon free will. This is regarded as the most perfect object of prophecy, because it is the most general and embraces all events that are in themselves unknowable.

God can enlighten the human mind in any way He pleases. He often makes use of angelic ministry in prophetic communications, or He Himself may speak to the prophet and illuminate his mind. Again the supernatural light of prophecy may be conveyed to the intellect or through the senses or the imagination. Prophecy may take place even when the senses are suspended in ecstasy, but this in mystical terminology is called rapture. St. Thomas teaches that there is no suspension of the sense activities when anything is presented to the mind of the prophet through impressions of the senses, nor is it necessary when the mind is immediately enlightened that activity of the senses should be suspended; but it is necessary that this should be the case when the manifestation is made by imaginative forms, at least at the moment of the vision or of the hearing of the revelation, because the mind is then abstracted from external things in order to fix itself entirely on the object manifested to the imagination. In such a case a perfect judgment cannot be formed of the prophetic vision during the transport of the soul, because then the senses which are necessary for a right understanding of things cannot act, and it is only when a man comes to himself and awakens from the ecstasy that he can properly know and discern the nature of his vision.[6]

FALSE PROPHETS, FANATICS, AND OTHER IMPOSTERS

In the modern world, you don't have to look far using news sources and historical writings to find accounts of madmen who claimed to hear the voice of God but proved to be false, as they intentionally exploited and at times murdered innocent human beings in the name of God. Some claim God spoke to them, some claim to be prophets of God, and yet others claimed to be Christ Himself. The work of the false prophet can also be identified in a few historic examples.

A sorcerer named of Bar-Jesus obstructed Paul and Barnabas in their attempts to bring divine illumination to a governor. Though Bar-Jesus was not stoned, he was named a false prophet in the Book of Acts, as his mission was the same as the prophet Moses warned of—to turn people away from God. Bar-Jesus was smitten for some time with blindness by the words of Paul.

Now when they had gone through the island to Paphos, they found a certain sorcerer, a false prophet, a Jew whose name was Bar-Jesus, who was with the proconsul, Sergius Paulus, an intelligent man. This man called for Barnabas and Saul and sought to hear the word of God. But Elymas the sorcerer (for so his name is translated) withstood them, seeking to turn the proconsul away from the faith.

Then Saul, who also is called Paul, filled with the Holy Spirit, looked intently at him and said, "O full of all deceit and all fraud, you son of the devil, you enemy of all righteousness, will you not cease perverting the straight ways of the Lord? And now, indeed, the hand of the Lord is upon you, and you shall be blind, not seeing the sun for a time."

And immediately a dark mist fell on him, and he went around seeking someone to lead him by the hand. Then the proconsul believed, when he saw what had been done, being astonished at the teaching of the Lord (Acts 13:6-12).

The definition of *Imposter*, given in the Catholic Dictionary, includes the following description:

St. Gregory of Tours tells us of a half crazy fanatic at the end of the sixth century who declared himself to be Christ and who traveled in the neighborhood of Arles in company with a woman whom he called Mary. He was declared to work miracles of healing and crowds of people believed in him and paid him Divine honor. In the end he moved about with a following of more than three thousand persons until he was killed in offering violence to an envoy of Bishop Aurelius. The woman named Mary under torture made a disclosure of all his frauds, but many of the populace still believed in them, and a number of other adventurers accompanied by hysterical prophetesses seem to have flourished in Gaul at the same epoch.

Throughout the Middle Ages we meet with many examples of such half crazy fanatics, and our imperfect information does not usually allow us to pronounce in what measure insanity or conscious fraud was responsible for their pretensions. Such cases are wont more particularly to be multiplied at times of national calamity or religious excitement. The epoch of the year 1000, owing to some vague expectation (an expectation, however, which has been much exaggerated), of the coming of the day of judgment (cf. Apoc. xx, 7) marked such a crisis, and Raoul Glaber (Migne, P. L., CXLII, 643-644) tells us in particular of two ecclesiastical agitators, one named Leotardus, at Châlons, and the other Wilgardus, at Ravenna, who at that time caused great disturbance. Leotardus pretended to have had extraordinary revelations and preached some sort of socialistic doctrine preventing the people from paying tithes. When his followers eventually deserted him he drowned himself in a well. Wilgardus appears to have been a literary fanatic who believed that he had been commanded by Virgil, Horace, and Juvenal in a vision to correct the dogmatic teaching of the Church. He had many followers and formed for a while a sort of schism until he was condemned by papal authority."[7]

Of course, there are many more accounts of impostors preying upon sincere, naïve believers throughout history. One thing that can be recognized in each of them is the desire to turn you away from your faith in God. The best way to know the true from the false is to judge as Christ taught: "*You will know them by their fruits...*" (Matt. 7:16). Or, as Paul said, "*But the fruit of the Spirit is love, joy, peace, longsuffering, kindness, goodness, faithfulness, gentleness, self-control...*" (Gal. 5:22-23).

The Voice of God Is For You

As you can see through this brief historical view, prophets have been around for a long time, and though the modern-day work does not serve the same purpose as it did thousands of years ago; it still exists and is meant to inspire you and equip you to learn to recognize when God is speaking to you. He wants to speak to you, not to make you some sort of freak to whom no one will listen, but to make you a blessing to your world.

On old world maps of earlier centuries, you will find symbols of sea serpents and other mythological creatures in the blank areas, denoting the danger of the unexplored or the unknown. On the Lenox Globe, the second oldest known terrestrial globe dating from 1503-07, you will find the inscription "Here be Dragons." These were meant to incite fear of the potential dangers of stepping outside the realm of the ordinary and the familiar, confining many of the otherwise adventurous hearts who desired to explore the world, to settle for merely dreaming and telling stories of others who took great risks and made history.

The fear of the unknown can be crippling and is many times propagated by the skeptics who hope to confine us to the boundaries of their own limited understanding and attempt to prevent a possible interruption in their fragile world by a discovery of something greater than they can explain.

However, the voice of the Creator cannot be eradicated, suppressed, or lost in the babblings of the skeptics. You and you alone can determine the outcome of your journey to encounter and explore the voice of God.

ENDNOTES

1. Ronald Reagan, second inaugural speech, http://www. reaganfoundation.org/reagan/speeches/speech.asp?spid=22.

2. "Prophecy," *The Catholic Encyclopedia*, http://www. newadvent.org/cathen/12473a.htm.

3. Winston Churchill, quoted in James C. Humes, *The Wit & Wisdom of Winston Churchill* (New York, NY: Harper Perennial, 1995).

4. Plato, "Apology," sct. 21, quoted in http://www.brainyquote. com/quotes/quotes/s/socrates133130.html.

5. George Mueller, quoted in http://www.higherpraise.com/illustrations/anxiety.htm.

6. St. Thomas Aquinas, quoted in "Prophecy," *The Catholic Encyclopedia*, http://www.newadvent.org/cathen/12473a.htm.

7. "Imposters," *The Catholic Encyclopedia*, http://www. newadvent.org/cathen/07698b.htm.

Chapter 5

How You Can Hear Him

L ISTEN! What do you hear? Nothing? Good. Now you are ready to hear the voice of God. You were created in the likeness and image of God, and this is in your blood, your bones, your heart, and your DNA. You may not always behave like God, certainly most of us don't think like Him, but we have the ability to hear God. Why would He create you for the sole purpose of friendship and relationship and then make it impossible for you to hear His voice? *He is speaking*, and because we don't recognize the simplicity of His mannerism and His appearance, we ignore it. The examples are clear in the ancient manuscripts. In the beginning, God created man in His image and likeness.

When you were born, and even before you were sent into this world, God placed a treasure in your heart. This treasure was positioned so that at the right moment, you are equipped with the tool you need to perform the extraordinary thing that you were born to perform; this is something that was meant for you only, and no one else can do it.

There are distinguishable features within each of us that from childhood indicate what that unique treasure is. It is amazing how this plays out in everyday life. My children are completely different from one another, and as they grow, I can see the qualities and features expressed from each of them individually, and I am amazed as I recognize what that treasure is.

The trouble is, we complicate matters when we force our choices on our children. Oftentimes they never discover the unique gift inside of them because of parents who have stifled their treasure through ancestral loyalty and transmissible tradition. Hereditary monarchy is at the base of this thinking; we feel that we have to hand down the inheritance of our fathers and forefathers to our children and then re-establish the inheritable rules.

Unfortunately, the religious system works this way today. Churches are filled with mass amounts of people in separate little groups, abiding by different sets of similar rules and laws that have nothing to do with their destiny or with seeing the truth. They are so focused on keeping the traditions of what they determined as God's inheritance, that there is no room for growth.

Jesus was angry with the religious leaders of His day when they tried to impose their inheritable rules on Him. Their attempt to enforce tradition on Jesus brought a familiar reaction from Him. He doesn't fit into a man-made mold. They challenged Jesus on irrelevant subjects and "fact," which was nothing more than a distraction to His mission and His destiny.

At that time Jesus went through the grain fields on the Sabbath. His disciples were hungry and began to pick some heads of grain and eat them. When the Pharisees saw this, they said to Him, "Look! Your disciples are doing what is unlawful on the Sabbath." He answered, "Haven't you read what David did when he and his companions were hungry? He entered the house of God, and he and his companions ate the consecrated bread – which was not lawful for them to do, but only for the priests. Or haven't you read in the Law that on the Sabbath the priests in the temple desecrate the day and yet are innocent? I tell you that one greater than the temple is here. If you had known what these words mean, 'I desire mercy, not sacrifice', you would not have condemned the innocent. For the Son of Man is Lord of the Sabbath (Matthew 12:1-9 NIV).

PERFORMANCE AND IDENTITY

Jesus not only challenged the Pharisees' triviality and pretentious claims with authentic facts, but He made sure that they knew who He was and that He was Lord over their claim. Forget for a moment that they were challenging His actions on the Sabbath, and rather see that their accusations were a distraction from a much bigger picture. This closed-minded pettiness distracted Christ from what was being formed in Him as the Son of God. He promptly replied, *"The Son of Man is Lord of the Sabbath."*

I love this response because He did not say I *am* Lord of the Sabbath, but referred to His name by transmittable title, imputed before birth. He *knows who He is*, and this challenged the Pharisees (religious system) because they couldn't fit Him into their religion and culture, thus losing the control they stubbornly refused to release. They were now placed in a position where they had to change their thinking and move out of their comfort zone—or get rid of Him.

Christ had to take His declaration to the next level, which was materialization and public demonstration. If He was successful at backing up His claim, a new set of rules and standards would emerge, giving life to a rejected, neglected, and spiritually disfigured generation. A religion that had become offensive was going to be redeemed by a man who had heard God's voice and believed it. The first account of Jesus ever hearing God's voice was when John baptized Him.

> *Then a voice came from heaven, "You are My beloved Son, in whom I am well pleased"* (Mark 1:11).

God spoke about Christ's destiny, but He also gave His personal approval *long before* Christ had succeeded in His mission in life. God spoke to Jesus based on who He was, not what He had done or was going to do. God does not judge you based on your performance. He has already made up His mind about you, and He speaks it right from the beginning.

Satan will search everywhere and look where he can, but the truth will only be revealed when the Father's voice is heard. When Jesus went out to meet satan, He had the Father's words as His defense. He told satan that He had nothing to prove because He knew who He was because of what the Father had told Him.

Jesus knew that His performance made no difference to what God thought about Him or what He thought about Himself. Performance helps and encourages, but it doesn't change who you are. You may make a mistake, but it doesn't change who you are.

You may fall to the ground, but it doesn't change who you are. You are who you are because He said so and that's who you are for eternity. American poet William Stafford wrote: "I have woven a parachute out of everything broken." Remember, any bad information you have about yourself is from forged documents.

> *Going on from that place, He went into their synagogue, and a man with a shriveled hand was there. Looking for a reason to accuse Jesus, they asked Him, "Is it lawful to heal on the Sabbath?" He said to them, "If any of you has a sheep and it falls into a pit on the Sabbath, will you not take hold of it and lift it out? How much more valuable is a man than a sheep! Therefore it is lawful to do good on the Sabbath." Then He said to the man, "Stretch out your hand." So he stretched it out and it was completely restored, just as sound as the other. But the Pharisees went out and plotted how they might kill Jesus (Matthew 12:9-14 NIV).*

Destroy Him? For obeying His predetermined destiny and doing good?!

FASHIONED BY HIS VOICE

Another example of this is when a little girl died and Jesus went to her house to pray for her. His language was not dictated by His surroundings, but by His DNA—the eternal factor.

> *When Jesus came into the ruler's house, and saw the flute players and the noisy crowd wailing, He said to them,*

*"Make room, for the girl is not dead, but sleeping." And they
ridiculed Him. But when the crowd was put outside, He
went in and took her by the hand, and the girl arose. And the
report of this went out into all that land"* (Matthew 9:23-
25).

They ridiculed Jesus because of His predestined disposition, so
He removed the distraction and did what He was capable of doing
under God's approval.

All of this sounds good, but if that specific calling or vocation
is not within the child's makeup, and not determined by those
genetic factors, they are then fashioned into something that they
cannot fit into.

God created the mold for each individual to fit into, and as we
grow and experience life, we are fashioned by His voice, which is
not always vocal; but as Shakespeare said, "My voice is my sword."[2]
Actions and events are often the clearest sounding words from
God's heart. He can be speaking to you through a billboard, a
movie, or a song. God is not human, but He is able to take the
human larynx and articulate His feelings to someone, or He can
choose a donkey, like He did with Balaam, to express His point of
view (see Num. 22:21-34).

He can speak in a still small voice, as He did with the Jewish
prophet Elijah (see 1 Kings 19:11). The great leader Moses discovered God's voice in a burning bush while walking on a mountain
(see Exod. 3:2-5). God will speak in different ways to everybody.
Nobody can really tell you exactly how to hear His voice. This is
the beauty of it, the discovery.

Touch the Sound

Your entire being actually hears God. The following passage is from "Touch the Sound," adapted from a talk by Evelyn Glennie, a deaf percussionist and musician:

> *Music is about listening. How are you going to hear this or that, if you're deaf? How do you hear it? I think I hear it through it my ears. But I also hear it through my head, my arms, my hands, cheekbones, my tummy, my legs and so on. Our lessons began with tuning a drum, to such a narrow pitch-interval, gradually changing the note. To open your hand up to each note, the difference is felt in the tiniest parts of your hand. Listening to the vibrations, connecting with sounds far more broadly than hearing with the ear. The ear is subject to a lot of things. The room, the type of drumsticks, the quality of the instrument; it all effects how we hear—different weight, different sound colors…we each have different sound colors. We all are human beings, each with different sound colors.*

When God spoke to Adam and Eve, they ran and hid themselves. This should not have been the case; however, their physical bodies and emotions reacted to the sound of God. The Israelites actually ran 16 miles when they heard God speaking from the mountain. Their entire beings were affected by that sound. Why were they so afraid? They were afraid because their view of God was so impaired and distorted by sin.

Jesus once made an adjustment to a blind man who, seeing people as trees, needed an alteration in his lens. Jesus asked the man, "Do you see anything?" and the man replied, "I see people;

they look like trees walking around." God will take the "anything" that you see and make the necessary adjustment, causing you to focus on the reality of humanity—the reason Jesus died—instead of the illusion continually presented by the world. The skill of the photographer lies, in part, in seeing something ordinary and making it extraordinary.

WHAT YOU SEE IS WHAT YOU HEAR

Someone once said, "You are evil because I am evil." To me, this means that because of the perversion and evil that is present in our minds, we see with the veil of that evil over our eyes. One of the greatest obstructions of spiritual justice is the religious mind-set, and this mind-set and culture has caused more pain than any other force. It controls the Church, the political world, families, marriages, relationships, and most importantly, our view of God. If your view of God is distorted, so will His voice be distorted. What you see is what you hear; what you perceive is what you hear.

If you see God as a sadistic taskmaster, then whatever He says to you will be received with that specific mind-set. Religion misrepresents God. It tames the Lion of Judah and displays God as a nasty old man with His only intention being to destroy you when you err.

I love the word *know*, and from God's perspective it relates to intimacy and deep knowledge gained between two human beings as a result of intercourse. Most people view this as physical, but it's not only physical, it is also an interchange of the entire being—spirit, soul, and body. It literally means, "to mingle with."

*Enoch lived sixty-five years, and begot Methuselah. After he begot Methuselah, **Enoch walked with God** three hundred years, and had sons and daughters. So all the days of Enoch were three hundred and sixty-five years. And **Enoch walked with God**; and he was not, for God took him* (Genesis 5:21-24, emphasis added).

Walking with God suggests closeness with God, as we would refer to a union of two people walking together in total agreement. The word *took* means "mingled with." Enoch was so close to God, in agreement and union, that He and God became one. Enoch walked with God and was no more, for God "mingled with" him.

For the kingdom of heaven is like a man traveling to a far country, who called his own servants and delivered his goods to them. And to one he gave five talents, to another two, and to another one, to each according to his own ability; and immediately he went on a journey. Then he who had received the five talents went and traded with them, and made another five talents. And likewise he who had received two gained two more also. But he who had received one went and dug in the ground, and hid his lord's money.

After a long time the lord of those servants came and settled accounts with them. So he who had received five talents came and brought five other talents, saying, "Lord, you delivered to me five talents; look, I have gained five more talents besides them." His lord said to him, "Well done, good and faithful servant; you were faithful over a few things, I will make you ruler over many things. Enter into the joy of your lord." He also who had received two talents came and said, "Lord, you delivered to me two talents; look, I have gained two more talents besides them." His lord said to him, "Well done, good and faithful servant; you have been faithful over a few things, I will make you ruler over many things. Enter into the joy of your lord."

Then he who had received the one talent came and said, "Lord, I knew you to be a hard man, reaping where you have not sown, and gathering where you have not scattered seed. And I was afraid, and went and hid your talent in the ground. Look, there you have what is yours." But his lord answered and said to him, "you wicked and lazy servant, you knew that I reap where I have not sown, and gather where I have not scattered seed. So you ought to have deposited my money with the bankers, and at my coming I would have received back my own with interest. So take the talent from him, and give it to him who has ten talents." For to everyone who has, more will be given, and he will have abundance; but from him who does not have, even what he has will be taken away (Matthew 25:14-29).

In this story, two other people were given an opportunity to double their venture and earn 100 percent of their investment, and they did. They were both serving the same Lord that the man with one talent was, and yet the latter "knew" his Lord as a hard man and therefore buried what was his only treasure. It's how he perceived his Lord that drove him to failure and lack; it was not his Lord's fault.

You cannot hear God if your perception or knowledge of Him is distorted. Marriages fail when the relationship is based on the physical aspect, and as they "walk" together, they discover that they are incompatible, spiritually and culturally, and they eventually walk away from each other when the mere physical side of their relationship is not enough to keep them together.

They don't "hear" each other anymore, and what was one becomes a divided mess, because the most powerful thing in a union of marriage is *procreation.* The word simply means to create and bring into being; to generate offspring.

Children are brought into this world, and then, when a marriage falls apart, the offspring (generation) are wounded and spiritually affected. Their relationship with God weakens because their view of a father and mother has been damaged, no matter how clean the divorce. Our view of God is first affected by our perception of family and relationships, and then second by the potentially ugly misrepresentation of God through religion.

People in the church have lost touch with the fact that our life in this relationship with Jesus is not on the descent, but on the ascent. The death of Christ paid for our sins, but it was His resurrection that gave life to our bodies. Religion embraces death sadistically, and it moves the risen Christ out of the Garden and back to the tomb. Religious people pray, praise (if they can), and walk and talk with a death mentality based on their relationship with Christ's death and not His resurrection. Many people keep referring to Him as the one still stuck on the Cross when in fact His greatest moment was in His resurrection. That is why religion stinks!

How Is God Speaking to You?

You are a unique copy of an ancient gift; you are a unique copy of an ancient manuscript, a unique copy of that which has taken place before. Ecclesiastes 1:9 says, "What has been will be again, what has been done will be done again; there is nothing new under the sun." So there is nothing new, but there is something uniquely copied from something ancient to make new. You must have something from the past that is relevant to your generation, in a unique form and expression. God can only bring forth truth in a delivery room setting, there's going to be pain, there's going to be labor and blood, but there will also be the sweet sound of life. You will hear the cry of a child; you will hear the truth that is relevant in this day and age.

You are a unique copy of an ancient gift of one of the many great men and women who walked this earth over time. Daniel, David, Isaiah, and so many more, all had a gift. When they died, their gift didn't die. The gift is alive to be used by each one of us. You are a unique copy of one of the greats. You are a unique copy of an ancient manuscript. Most people don't want to think of themselves as a copy, but the word *unique* will refresh that feeling. Unique means that you are worthy of being considered in a class by yourself. What is your unique expression?

> *And Elisha said, "As the Lord of hosts lives, before whom I stand, surely were it not that I regard the presence of Jehoshaphat king of Judah, I would not look at you, nor see you. But now bring me a musician." Then it happened, when the musician played, that the hand of the Lord came upon him. And he said, "Thus says the Lord: 'Make this valley full of ditches'"* (2 Kings 2:14-16).

Elisha was completely dull of hearing, until they brought a guitarist. He told them to bring him a musician because he was not hearing anything. Most of the messianic songs and prophecies in the Psalms were given through music. I need music to reach my full expression. It's my inspiration, which is why you will see me with a full band behind me, inspiring me to hear. This is my unique expression.

Each of us has a unique expression; therefore, God speaks to us according to the unique characteristics He placed inside of us before we were born. One type of person may be cautious, not eager to take risks, while another type of person craves adventure and new things. Another may be more of a socialite, enjoying the company of other people, while another type prefers to be alone. God created us this way for diversity and excitement. Different personalities compliment each other.

This is especially true in a marriage or any type of partnership. Each personality has its strengths and weaknesses. God speaks to us according to our type. He recognizes and takes into account culture, personality, history, and family. For example, with my five children, I have to speak to each one of them according to their personality in order to be most effective. With my little girl, I would usually have to carry through the threat of a punishment, whereas with my little boy, the threat was usually enough for him to adjust his behavior.

This is only an example of discipline, but the same goes in caring for them. Jane and I both know that in speaking to our five uniquely different children, we have to adjust our tone and presentation for each one. We do this because we love them, and love understands them as they are. God does the same with each of us. He made us who we are with our unique characteristics and personalities; therefore he speaks to us according to who we are and the personality He gave us.

It is intriguing to consider how God has designed your unique temperament and personality to suit His expression through you. You do not lose your unique, God-given personality when He speaks to and through you, but He liberates it as an expression of His perfect love. Therefore, we must look at how God's design for your life influences the nature of His communication with you.

Let's look at the ancient manuscripts to see how God spoke over the ages to four of the most influential men in history—the great leader Moses; Saul of Tarsus who killed hundreds of thousands of Christians; Abraham, the father of many nations; and Peter, one of Jesus' closest friends and followers.

Consider Moses. He needed clarity and certainty. He saw a burning bush and heard an audible voice. He held a stick that became a snake and a snake that turned into a stick. He watched as his own hand miraculously turned leprous then turned back to normal living tissue as a sign to the people. After seeing all these things, he still tried to talk his way out of the assignment God gave him because of his self-consciousness over his speech impediment (see Exod. 3-4). Nonetheless, God spoke to him in the language he needed to hear. This is what love does; it speaks in the language that is understood by the hearer. God understands that some people, like Moses, need certainty, and He will speak to you accordingly.

Saul, a very strong personality, encountered another expression of God's communication. He was persecuting Christians until he came face to face with God, who knocked him off his donkey and caused him to go blind. When Saul was brought down to a vulnerable position, Jesus began a cordial conversation with him.

Saul, soon to be called Paul, has the type of temperament that really only wants to know one thing in any new situation—who is in charge? So he carefully poses a question as he is lying on the ground: "Who are you, Lord?" (See Acts 9:1-19.)

One can only imagine the sense of deep dread that must have swept over him when he heard: "I am Jesus, the One you are persecuting!" Can you imagine what a feeling of utter terror it must have been for Saul to come to the realization that the work he had been doing, convinced it was the work of God, had been taken quite personally by the awesome supernatural being who now stood before him in a blinding light? It took a drastic act of being blinded by the Light for Paul to see and *hear*.

God spoke to Abraham and told him he would become a father to many nations, and He also spoke about the great covenant friendship that He would have with Abraham (see Gen. 17:1-8). God called Abraham His friend. Many of you have a need for connection, like Abraham, and God understands that. He entrusted to Abraham the role of "father." Abraham avoided all conflict and strife in his life. This is why we see many millions of Arabs surrounding a few million Jews in Israel. The one called the great father, Abraham, did not want to fight with his wife about a son, so he fathered Ishmael through another source (see Gen. 16:1-4). God spoke to Abraham in a nurturing way, which is the only way he would have understood.

Peter, on the other hand, represents the communication and persuasion capacity that is found in the make-up of men and women. One moment Peter's words are bringing him special affirmation for his ability to hear God reveal Jesus' identity (see Matt. 16:15-17); and not long after, he is cursing like a drunken sailor in order to avoid the painful consequences of association with Jesus (see Matt. 26:74). Other times, however, it was Peter's voice that would rise as the spokesman for the others. Whenever the disciples were all together, 70 percent of the dialogue that has been recorded involves Peter. This type of temperament has a need for significance through the recognition that comes from their peers, and God knows this about them. Perhaps this is why Jesus personally restored Peter and reinstated him in the presence of his peers (see John 21:15-19).

Peter was one of those people who had a tendency to say the wrong thing at the wrong time. He was impulsive. He acted without thinking, which was good and bad, depending on the action. Peter also experienced *quickening*. These are feelings many of us experience. Impulse is something prompted out of a need to be accepted, recognized, and loved. Impulse pushes you to do it now so you can get what you want right now. Quickening is when the Spirit, without you specifically having a need, quickens or puts a spiritual impulse into you to do something or say something. When it passes your mental capacity, it passes your need, whatever it may be, and you just do it.

One day Jesus is with His disciples and He asks them a question, "Who do men say that I am?" The disciples thought about it a few seconds and then began to offer their opinions and started quoting what some of the public were saying. Jesus had heard enough of the "*some sayers*." He said, "That is what *some* say, now who do you say that I am?" The disciples fell silent because they were afraid to say what they thought in case they were wrong. They were afraid to get out of the box of public opinion.

Suddenly there was a *quickening* that came upon Peter and he ignored the possibility of being wrong. He says, "You are the Christ, the son of the living God." Jesus immediately turns to him and responds to the quickening of the Spirit in Peter and says, "Flesh and blood did not reveal this to you but My Father who is in Heaven." Then He goes on to bless Peter for His response to the quickening (see Matt. 16:17). But Peter also acted on impulse and when he tried to stop Jesus from speaking about his death on the Cross, Jesus actually rebuked him for speaking as the enemy (see Matt. 16:23).

God created our human nature and gave it to us as part of our makeup. It's beautiful to see how our instinct to love and feel comes from within. There is nothing evil within the nature God placed inside each of us. However, evil can influence and taint what God intended for good.

Personally, I have an impatient nature, which is beneficial when I'm standing in front of someone hearing something about their future and I just spit it out without thinking about the consequences of it being wrong. On the other hand, when I'm impatient in my home, my wife gets extremely frustrated and says I finish all of her sentences before she has a chance to get her point across. Of course, I'm making light of it, but this is true in many situations. You're going to lose your temper and get angry, it's human nature; but if you allow evil to come and use this in a negative way, you could hurt yourself and others.

Breaking the Power of Self-Prejudice

One of the biggest problems we encounter on our journey to our future is a thing called self-prejudice. Self-prejudice simply means that you do not believe that God believes in you or what He believes about you. Your judgment of yourself is usually more difficult to overcome than someone else's judgment of you.

This is the biggest problem I have when I am delivering an utterance to someone. They just cannot believe that God thinks enough of them to take the time to speak to them, yet alone that He has words of affirmation and approval for them. The first thing that I do is I tell them that God loves them just the way they are, and He thinks they are beautiful. Most people look at me and think that I have lost my mind. It's almost impossible for someone to believe those words after a life of being beaten down with words of defeat and failure.

But I'm not seeing them as they are standing in front of me, I'm seeing them exactly as God does, seeing that treasure deep inside that needs to come forth. Don't think that this is a modern problem. When the prophet Samuel told Saul that he would rule over Israel and that he was the desire of Israel, Saul responded by saying that he was "only a Benjamite" (see 1 Sam. 9:21). Self-prejudice drove him to that place. He couldn't believe that he was the one chosen. That insecurity would follow him all the days of his life and ultimately keep him from his future, from fulfilling his destiny.

Moses, Gideon, and even David struggled with self-prejudice. David went so far as to speak to himself, asking his soul why he was so discouraged, trying to encourage himself in the words God spoke into his life (see Ps. 42). Don't allow your self-prejudice attitude to dictate your future and destiny.

Sometimes self-prejudice affects the way God speaks to us. Too often God has to speak to us through dreams because our shame and insecurities won't allow Him to get a word through to us face to face. Most people, when they are conscious, are focused on their needs and their pain, and these things dictate their perspective, so God will speak to them through a dream when they are not so aware of these things.

HEARING THE DIVINE WHISPER

God wants to help each of us grow in our communion with Him and understand that many things we may dismiss as fleeting, spontaneous thoughts or daydreams, may be actual images from Him, which He is using to communicate with us or initiate interaction. Often the ability to understand this is developed through prayer. As your mind seemingly wanders, it may actually be pollinating like a bee, touching on matters too difficult to access with our minds alone.

When operating in my gift, I frequently see faces or pictures or even cartoons that convey very clear messages, such as names, locations, or events taking place surrounding the person that God is using me to speak to. For instance, I was standing in front of a woman and I saw Garfield the cat in my mind, so I quickly said the word Garfield. Her response revealed that Garfield was the name of the person she was praying for.

God doesn't say much because He doesn't need to. All He has to do is say one word, and it's up to you to fill in the rest of the sentence. If the sentence is incorrect, God erases it and you start over again. If God whispers, "prosperity," you have the choice to write, "...will destroy me with greed and pride," or you can choose to write, "...will delight God, and I will be empowered to assist humanity and extend His Kingdom." When God speaks to you, and you act upon it, a force of progressive revelation takes over.

God's voice is less frequently heard through the ear, although this can and does happen. Most of the time, however, you will hear Him through His "still, small voice," as Elijah did (see 1 Kings 19:11). Many people wonder if the voice they hear is actually God or just their own voice, because what they hear sounds familiar, like their own voice.

Auditory sounds are not limited to words. I often hear and see things that are not verbal, yet they are God's communication to me. For instance, I once stood before a man in Detroit who really needed help, but I also knew he needed to know I was "for real." As I stood in front of him, I heard the sound of birds in my right ear, and in an instant I heard the word "doctor," so I knew this man was named Dr. Bird. I called him Dr. Bird, and since nobody in the room knew his identity, this was a special sign to him that what I said could be trusted.

Kinesthetic sensing is a modern term for discerning divine communications through physical sensation. It is a fascinating way to hear God. This involves movement, fragrances, temperature changes, and feelings of pain and other sensations. I sometimes feel the temperature change around my body as I enter a moment in someone's past when they experienced a traumatic event. Similarly, I may feel heat, which can have several meanings, from an inspiration to minister to someone, to the presence of an angel. Likewise, I sometimes smell a fragrance or a stench, and these sensations also tell me something about the person I am standing in front of.

The creative ways through which God may choose to speak to us cannot all be summed up or taught in a book by anyone. Many are longing to hear God and yet feel He is not speaking, when in fact He is actually speaking in numerous ways that they do not yet recognize. When God speaks to you, He will speak in a familiar voice. It will come from within you. We should be listening and feeling and looking within, and the reason I say that is because when God speaks to you, you don't just hear a voice or see an image or feel a feeling. When God speaks, you hear and see and feel and understand all at once.

IT'S COMING FROM WITHIN

God can speak to us in any way He chooses, but He will most frequently speak to us from within. Expect God to speak to you in the secret place of your innermost being—your spirit.

When Adam and Eve heard the sound of the Lord God walking in the Garden, they hid themselves. One of the reasons for their attempt to hide was that God had become an unperceived sound to them, and He was no longer a clear voice. As human beings, it is our nature to run away from things that are not familiar to us. We fear what we do not understand, and because of the shift after Adam and Eve disobeyed, God's voice was no longer a voice; it had become just a sound (see Gen. 3:8).

God's voice has been speaking throughout human history. As you know, this began at creation. God spoke light into existence (see Gen. 1:14). His voice, always creative, is still speaking today. One of the basic principles of prophecy is that God's voice creates something new in our lives. God supplies us with direction, guidance, and knowledge; He created us with His words and His breath—the breath of life, which keeps us going. His intention for us is the same intention He had for Adam and Eve—to have dominion over the earth and to fill it with righteousness (see Gen. 1:28). When the wind of God comes to you, it has to contain His voice before any purpose can come out of it.

Every day, as you hear God's voice, your knowledge, wisdom, power, and abundance will increase. More importantly, God's character will be formed in you.

If humankind had continued to hear the voice of God, as Adam and Eve had in the beginning, we would be secure and creative beings who would possess the ability to take dominion over all things. After Adam fell, though, the voice of God was no longer a delight to his ear or a joy to his heart. It was terrifying to him, because his own nature had changed from one of innocence and righteousness to evil.

"So then faith comes by hearing, and hearing by the word of God" (Rom. 10:17). Satan understands the power of faith, and this is why he constantly attacks us with an awareness of sin—so we will not hear God's voice; or if we do, we will be afraid of Him. God speaks as a friend, not to judge and ridicule, but to love and protect.

KEEP YOUR EYES OPEN

Don't miss His voice. Sometimes you have to recognize His form before you can hear Him. Moses walked by the burning bush once without noticing anything significant about it; but then he looked again and saw that it was God, and *then* he heard God's voice. The process of recognizing God's form may well result in a challenge for you, because the vessel, method, or voice God has chosen may not be the method you desire. A man named Balaam was approached by an ass and would have never expected God's voice to come from it; but he recognized God and then heard His voice, even through an ass. God will show up—however and wherever He likes, and you need to make sure you don't miss Him.

This is very important for us to understand, because if we don't recognize Him, we will miss Him. When Jesus walked on the water toward the disciples, the storm had affected them so greatly that, when they saw Him, they said it was a ghost. He was right there, but the Bible actually says that they didn't recognize Him because He was in a place that they *least expected Him* (see Mark 6:48-50). God will often come to us when we least expect it and will say things we least expect.

Hearing God can be compared with listening to a radio. The old radios had a knob and had to be tuned into a particular radio station. With the advance of technology, we no longer have to tune in. But with God, you have to tune in to His voice. He's always speaking; we just have to find the right radio wave to hear His voice. God doesn't suddenly start speaking. His word is already in the atmosphere, and it is up to us to tune in.

The God of the universe may be talking to you in ways you don't perceive, especially when your needs for connection, accomplishment, recognition, or certainty are being met. When you really understand this, you can graduate to an even higher level where God will speak through you as an oracle in order to encourage others in the exact language they most readily understand.

Chapter 6

Optical Fusion

THERE are three levels of seeing that you need to possess in order to have complete knowledge in your life: sight, insight, and foresight. They are your pathways to complete knowledge. *Sight* is your natural field of vision or the way you see things through your natural eyes. It's the way you see yourself today in your present circumstances and surroundings. *Insight* is an extension of your natural field of vision and the capacity to see further and to discern the true nature of a situation. Insight means we detect by senses other than natural vision, and it allows us to grasp the hidden nature of things.

The third level in gaining complete knowledge is *foresight*, the perception of events before they occur. Foresight is your ability to see beyond your present and into your future—and to see what God sees. It is the highest degree of prophetic vision and allows you to begin acting in reference to the future.

When Adam and Eve "fell" in the Garden, the manuscripts say "their eyes were opened" (see Gen. 3:7). Of course their eyes were open up to that point, but God was speaking about their natural sight. Everything was perfect without sin. Before they sinned, they were seeing what God saw, with insight and foresight. After they sinned, their eyes were opened, and they were seeing with their natural field of vision—they saw themselves naked, and they hid. They could no longer see themselves with their spiritual eyes as God saw them, and they were ashamed.

When you take your eyes off your nakedness and failure, insight provides identity, and foresight provides destiny, which are the two keys to living a prophetic lifestyle. Insight and foresight drive you away from sinning, and even if you still stumble, they will drive you to overcome. They allow you to see your end result, your "happily ever after," and that gives you the power to make it through whatever is thrown at you.

When you only see with your natural sight, you are aware of your circumstances and situational problems, and they dictate your actions and your behavior. If you can see with your spiritual eyes, you are able to overcome your present circumstance. Foresight makes you act in reference to the future, behaving as though your future is now.

Unfortunately, most people do not operate by foresight because it's just too difficult to believe against the circumstances. Like Adam and Eve, their eyes were opened, their natural field of vision is controlled by their circumstances, and they see that they are naked so they hide.

Don't hide! Let the prophetic carry you to your place of destiny and victory. Let insight and foresight be your greatest guide. With natural vision, one only sees the risk, but with insight, the prophetic person sees the reward, and I have learned that the reward is worth the risk.

GOD SPEAKS IN REFERENCE TO THE FUTURE

When God talks to you, He talks in reference to your future. He is not deterred by your present circumstances. He sees your future. When God spoke to Jacob, one of the founders of the Jewish nation, He spoke to His future (just like He did to his grandfather Abraham). God did not deal with Jacob according to his lying nature and unscrupulous ways. None of us would have chosen this deceiving character; he had serious character flaws. But God has a different set of eyes than you and I do. He has an eye on Jacob's future, not his past or present. God was able to see that Israel was in his loins, and He spoke to his destiny (see Gen. 28:13-15).

That is one of the great problems in the Church. We are guilty of judging people according to their past and present circumstances. We then lock them in with our judgments. The goal of the prophet is to release people from the prison of self-judgment and the judgment of others so that they can begin to live in their future.

God has a whole new world for you to see and experience. To get there, you will have to leave the valley of natural sight and ascend to the high places where God will show you the destiny that awaits you. It's a whole new world, and it's so exciting. It's dangerous, risky, radical, revolutionary, and chaotic, but it's great! Chaotic, yes, but it is an ordered chaos that will bring you to your destiny.

You must tune out the other voices in your ear that are telling you that you are a failure and that you will never succeed. You have to hear the Voice that is speaking to you about your successful future and your destiny in Him.

Jacob's son, Joseph, looked into the future and saw his destiny; he would be a ruler in Israel and his brothers would one day bow before him. However, the pathway to his destiny was not an easy one. It was a pathway filled with pain, as is true for most of God's prophets. When Joseph was thrown into an Egyptian prison, there was chaos in his spirit, but it was perfectly ordered by God. He would not stay in that prison for long. He saw the future, his future. The Voice gave him hope and courage.

In January 1994, I was in San Juan Capistrano, California, performing at a church in the area. My wife and children and beloved mother-in-law, Gloria Barnes, were there. Gloria has been a prayer warrior, support, and lifeline to our ministry since it was launched in 1978. I turned to her in that meeting and said these words; "Gloria you will live to a ripe old age just like Abraham." There were many other aspects to the prophecy, but what stood out to us was that she was to live a long life for a greater purpose.

In May of that same year, after she had flown back to her homeland, South Africa, we heard news that she had contracted Meningitis and it had not been discovered for three days. By the time she reached the hospital, she fell into a coma and the doctors pronounced her brain dead.

They tried to revive her after she flat-lined three times, and after the third time she came back to life only to be thrust into a deeper coma. My wife, Jane, came to me in tears and asked me what I felt about her situation. She was pregnant and on the other side of the world, which made her feel helpless. I told her that I would pray, and I spent the early hours of the morning deep in prayer.

At around 4:00 A.M., I was reminded of the promise that had already been given and the record set for her life. Immediately, I remembered the words I spoke to her months before, and I found them and printed it out for Jane and the family. Jane asked me what I saw, and I responded immediately, "She will fully recover with no sign of brain damage. The only thing that I see is that she will walk with a limp, but without need of a cane."

Jane flew to South Africa with my son Caleb, who was only a little boy at the time, and before they left I prayed over a handkerchief and put it into his little hand and said, "Take this to Granny and tell her she will be healed."

When Jane arrived at the hospital in South Africa, she found a morbid, deathly spirit over the family and loved ones who had already accepted her mother's death. She took Caleb and placed him on the hospital bed. He draped the cloth over her and made the pronouncement I had told him to make.

Gloria Barnes came out of her coma, defying every prognosis and shortsightedness; and lives today, perfectly normal with a slight limp. The Word of the Lord released foresight in a prophetic word, and when Jane and Caleb arrived at the hospital, the necessary spiritual components connected Gloria Barnes to her destiny.

What is your perspective of a situation? What are you seeing about your circumstance? You've just been told you have a growth in your body. What do you do? Do you succumb to fear? Do you blame God? Do you give up? Do you live by your natural field of vision and run and hide? Or, will you rise up and operate with insight and foresight and act in deference to the future?

If you live by insight, you look beyond what the doctors are telling you and you live by what God is telling you. Foresight will give you knowledge into your future to know the truth of a situation. God reveals the truth to us, and sometimes the facts aren't the truth. In other words, the doctors may be giving you the facts about your situation, but God is giving you the truth of the situation. The whole struggle is really fact versus truth.

We must not allow ourselves to be confused by the "facts;" we must always hold on to the truth that God gives us through His promise. Although you may know the facts, if you know the truth, then you have the ability to see yourself in the future. If you can see yourself in the future, then you will overcome your present problem and get there!

HOW DO YOU SEE THINGS?

Monet, the well-known impressionist painter, said that he wished he had been born blind and later gained sight. That way he would be able to look at the world free of the knowledge of what the objects were so that he could more fully appreciate their color.

Sight brings knowledge. Adam and Eve in the Garden obeyed the voice of carnal desire and the Bible says "their eyes were opened"—apparently Monet was not far from the truth. They were blind to the knowledge of objects, and thereby appreciated the colors or the sounds of God. Objects seem to take our attention away and blind us oftentimes to the beauty that surrounds them. The word *object* means "something perceptible by one or more of the senses, especially by vision or touch; a material thing; a focus of attention, feeling, thought or action; the purpose, aim or goal of a specific action or effort."

What I came to realize was that with an object came a focus on one particular subject, and everything else was dimmed or out of sight. While focusing on one object, you become subject to it, and therefore, insight and foresight are overshadowed by sight, which is extremely limited. To *be subjective* means "existing in the mind; belonging to the thinking subject; placing excessive emphasis on one's own moods, attitudes, opinions, etc; unduly egocentric."

So our enemy keeps our attention on an object—something perceptible by vision or touch, something material—and we become subjective. Our minds are controlled by and focus on ourselves, our attitudes and opinions, etc. That is why I am a firm believer that we are only able to use a small percentage of our brain, because we are controlled by natural vision and not by soul and spirit vision. We are fed information by objects and subjects so that our attention is controlled by what we see and think only.

Humankind has rejected the idea that the Spirit world has any more to offer than ghosts, demons, fairies, and such. You only have to look at what Hollywood releases annually about the spirit world and you'll realize that there is a severe ignorance regarding the Spirit world or the heavenlies. Organized religion is subject to objects and it takes objection to any proposal on the subject of an ordered chaos outside of its controlled world. The religious focus on (and keep everyone under their leadership focused on) petty matters that steer them away from divine relationship.

In the early 1970s, while the church was measuring the length of skirts and the length of hair, men were pioneering a way to communicate through the Internet; because of their foresight, they became the pioneers of "Windows," Microsoft's own version of the graphical user interface (GUI) for computers. Windows offered an alternative to the non-user friendly DOS command prompt and positioned Microsoft to compete with other systems on the market that employed a GUI.

The release of Windows 3.0 in 1990 was a huge success, selling close to ten million copies in just two years. By continuing to ensure that most computers came with Microsoft software pre-installed, the Microsoft Corporation became the largest software company in the world, earning Bill Gates a place in *Forbes* magazine as the wealthiest person in the world for several years. Bill Gates is a billionaire today, and the church still struggles to raise money—as my friend Johnny Caswell said, "trying to sell Melba toast when everyone wants beer."

BELIEVING IS SEEING

I have not seen, but I have been shown.

To *see* is: "To look at with the eyes, visible recognition." When I see something, I grow acquainted with its form, shape, and sound because it's within seeing and hearing distance.

To *show* is: "To indicate, to serve as a sign; to make evident by *expression*."

The majority of people prefer a visual image to a visual sense or sensation. It would be so much easier if we could see the entire picture with clarity, where no faith is involved. Visual estimation is another description for visual sense. It could be a vague impression or realization. A sense of security means that you are visually sensing something, but you don't necessarily have a visual image of the security that you sense. God is most pleased when we use faith (see Heb. 11:6). There is a difference between the two degrees of sight.

We say, "seeing is believing," because when a thing appears, there is evidence of its existence. However, seeing is *not* believing—in reality, believing is seeing.

Biologist and author Lyall Watson wrote: *I wouldn't have believed it if I hadn't seen it, but more neuro-physiologically precise to say I wouldn't have seen it at all, if I hadn't already believed it in the first place.*

Once you are shown something, you have to believe in it before it can be seen. When God speaks and shows you something (remembering now that it is an indication or sense rather than a visual connection) the next thing that happens to you is conceptualization—forming it into a concept in order to explain it. This is impossible, and even though unavoidable, it can be detrimental if it draws you away from the original perception. This will also help a lot of people to understand why they don't hear clearly. Most of the time they don't *hear* clearly because they are relying on the tympanic membrane, better known as the eardrum, to listen instead of hearing with the spiritual ear, which is sense, realization, impression.

Remember that when you are *shown* something, it comes by expression or guidance and not necessarily through visual contact.

An example from the manuscripts follows. Samuel the prophet, under the command of God, prepared a dinner for a special guest, a man named Saul. Samuel had not *seen*, but had been *shown*:

Now the Lord had told Samuel in his ear the day before Saul came, saying, "Tomorrow about this time I will send you a man from the land of Benjamin, and you shall anoint him commander over My people Israel, that he may save My people from the hand of the Philistines; for I have looked upon My people, because their cry has come to Me." So when Samuel saw Saul, the Lord said to him, "There he is, the man of whom I spoke to you. This one shall reign over My people" (1 Samuel 9:15-17).

The Lord told Samuel *in his ear*, the day before Saul came, saying: "*Tomorrow about this time I will send you a man from the land of Benjamin, and you shall anoint him King over My people Israel.*" So when Samuel saw (visual image), the Lord said to him, "*There he is, the man of whom I spoke to you. This one shall reign over My people.*"

Samuel was shown before he saw. You will be shown before you see it in reality, and then you will recognize what you were shown, and the inner voice of God will have to point it out. Most people have actually heard Him, but they don't realize it because they are listening too hard. God will show you so that you can see and ultimately operate in the three levels of sight as discussed earlier in the chapter.

THE MIND AND THE SENSES

Humans are not merely physical beings but also spirit and soul. Thus, to access our prophetic faculties, there are two areas of our being that must connect with our spirit (heart), since this is where the hidden truth and treasures lie:

1. The mind (subjective).

2. The sense (objective).

If the mind and the senses do not connect with our spirits, everything decelerates, thereby slowing down the rate of advancement in science, knowledge, and the world in general. The only reason that things have increased at a higher rate of velocity in the past century is because the Kingdom of God has advanced outside of the four walls of religion. Today people are more open to spiritual things and even though severely attacked, God is the most sought after being on the earth.

In the manuscripts, Solomon, the writer of Proverbs, said, "*Where there is no vision [progressive spiritual revelation] the people perish*" (Prov. 29:18 KJV). The Hebrew word *Parah*, means "to decay, decelerate, go backward, diminish." We have seen a moral decline in the world because of the lack of progressive truth, which is attained by foresight; without foresight, the vision in humans diminishes causing people to regress morally and spiritually.

Every day there should be a development of your personality and occupation and the fulfillment of each of your talents and abilities. You will recognize having done this by improvement in these three areas:

1. Clarity of thinking and perception,

2. Advancement of your judgment,

3. Self-control.

Instead of always trying to recapture the past in order to keep it in your existence, capture the future to bring it into your existence now!

THE TWO TRUTHS

Without the force of God, which is righteousness, peace, joy, eternity, etc., truth is only available through illegal means and eventually destroys lives because of corruption—perversion of integrity, morality, and a debased form of the original facts. Austrian philosopher Ludwig Wittgenstein wrote, "Those who try to tell the truth are spies without passwords, smuggling bits of silence past the sentries."

Physicist Leo Szilard once announced to his friend, Hans Bethe, that he was thinking of keeping a diary: "I don't intend to publish it: I am merely going to record the facts for the information of God."

"Don't you think God knows the facts?" Bethe asked. "Yes," said Szilard. "He knows the facts, but He does not know *this* version of the facts."

There are indeed two versions of the facts—the pure and the corrupt. But before we waste any more time with these obvious facts, let me show you the dimensions of truth that exist.

There are *two dimensions of truth* that exist and are attainable—historical truth and creative truth. One is based on history and the other is based upon the future. One is visible and the other is invisible but within our reach *and* in existence. *Truth in the*

tomb *is not exactly like truth in the **womb**.* One is present whether objective or subjective, and the other is invisibly present.

For us to argue that a child is nonexistent in a six-month pregnant mother because the child is unseen and the only proof is the mother's increase in size, is as stupid as saying that there is no wind simply because the only proof we see are the leaves moving on the trees. Truth only reveals itself in purity when one gives up all preconceived ideas. That's why a prophetic voice is so important to the world—it shatters preconceived ideas, having had a glimpse of the future. Please notice, it is only a glimpse. This is like the camera that captures one shot in a dark place and has to tell the story based on that *one flash of light* which is then developed in a dark room in order for the world to see the little bit that was revealed. However, it is enough to break any presuppositions and preconceived ideas. The problem: there are too many opinionated people.

Paul, the writer of three quarters of the New Testament, says: *"For it is God who commanded light to shine out of darkness, who has shone in our hearts to give the light of the knowledge of the Glory of God..."* (2 Cor. 4:6). The word dark here denotes "unknown." Therefore, when you are in an unknown place you are in darkness. The darkness does *not* speak of sin necessarily but a place where you cannot see with your present light (understanding, illumination).

If God has placed eternity in our hearts, which is what Solomon says (see Eccles. 3:11), then we need to clarify what eternity is. It is a state of eternal existence, and my own personal belief is that it is past and future inside each man and woman. The past is with us, and there are times when a gentle reminder through a song, a fragrance, or a picture can take us right back to that place. It's as though we are reliving the entire moment. How could it be so powerful? Because it is still within your eternal existence.

However the future is just as powerful, and it's only because of the unknown factor that we refuse to delve into it. According to apostle Paul, God commanded light (illumination and understanding) to shine out of darkness (the unknown realm or the *future*). He goes on to say that this light has shone in our hearts to *give* the light. We carry the future inside of us, and yet, because of it we are afraid to enter the unknown to get a glimpse of it. Instead, we look away and remain under the control of memories and historical truth. Truth in the womb is unknown.

Today we have modern medical equipment to see the unborn child—ultrasound. Ultrasound is sound with a frequency greater than the upper limit of human hearing. Some animals such as dogs, dolphins, bats, and mice, have an upper frequency limit that is greater than that of the human ear, which acts as a low-pass filter. This frequency limit in humans is caused by the middle ear, which acts as a low-pass filter. If ultrasound is fed directly into the skull bone and reaches the cochlea without passing through the middle ear, much higher frequencies (up to about 200 kHz) can be heard. This effect, sometimes called ultrasonic hearing, was first discovered by divers exposed to a high-frequency (ca. 50 kHz) sonar signal.

Some have said that children can hear some high-pitched sounds that older adults cannot hear, as in humans the upper limit pitch of hearing gets lower with age. A cell phone company has used this anomaly to create ring signals heard only by young people. Hence, I believe that childlikeness *enhances our hearing to the degree we can see beyond this realm and into the future.*

Medical sonography (ultrasonography) is an ultrasound-based diagnostic medical imaging technique used to visualize muscles, tendons, and many internal organs, their size, structure, and any pathological lesions. They are also used to visualize a fetus during routine and emergency prenatal care. Obstetric sonography is commonly used during pregnancy.

As with the ultrasound, once we catch a glimpse of that which is in darkness, we are able to describe the various features, albeit with limitations. There are certain things that cannot be learned but only revealed. There are many exciting treasures that are present, within our reach but outside the range of natural apprehension and can only be known by spiritual comprehension. Whatever is ahead of you is invisible, but it is *present* and waiting to be uncovered. You have the power to make good history!

Winston Churchill said, "History will be kind to me because I'm making it!" Remember, only you can shape and fashion what is in your future.

OPTICAL FUSION

We have already explained why sight is one of the secrets of hearing God. That is why prophets are often called *seers*. When people talk about the prophetic, they are usually referring to hearing the voice of God, but sight is the great key of the prophet. Before there is hearing, there is seeing. The oracles of God are able to speak because *they have seen*. Before there can be a word, there is a thought, a creative thought generated by what one has seen.

Abraham Heschel, the Jewish philosopher who was an active participant in the Civil Rights movement in the 1960s, told his daughter that, "Words create worlds."[1] Before God spoke the word in the beginning of time, He had a thought based upon what He saw in the future. He had seen a world that would become our world. Out of what He had seen, He spoke the word, and that word became a world—our world. That is the power of the prophet. He sees a world envisioned by God, and what he sees brings forth words, and those words create a world for others.

When God gave you two eyes, He did not mean that your eyes would control your natural field of vision. You've got to have the sight of the eyes. I am not talking about *natural sight* but about a new set of eyes that can see the invisible. As my friend, Oral Roberts says, "*Once you see the invisible, you can do the impossible.*"

Let me explain. Better is the sight of the eyes. I am talking about eyes that have a greater field of vision—a vision that exists within you. I am referring to your spiritual eyes that are capable of seeing into the spiritual dimension. To be a prophet you need a new set of eyes to see what God sees. This is the power of the oracle.

> *I was in the Spirit on the Lord's Day, and I heard behind me a loud voice like the sound of a trumpet...I turned to **see the voice** that was speaking with me...* (Revelation 1:10,12 NASB, emphasis added).

John, one of Jesus' best friends, was a seer and a prophet of God. He had eyes that saw the voice. Isn't that interesting? He turned to *see* the voice, not to *hear* the voice. To see the hidden things of the spiritual realm, as John saw, you need *optical fusion*, a fusion of sight. John was about to see what God sees, but it would it would be through his eyes.

Optical fusion is the combining of images from two eyes to form a single visual percept. In other words, there are two sights that must be combined, *God's sight and your sight.* And the beautiful thing about optical fusion is that God needs your sight. God needs your vision to perform the impossible.

In His communication with Jeremiah, another great prophet, He shows him some of the crazy things that Jeremiah is going to do in his life. He told Jeremiah that he would be an influential voice to nations and that his task would be to "cause chaos to bring order"—to shake nations out of their complacency and steer them in the right direction. Jeremiah refused to believe these words and complained to God: "Ah, God, I am a youth, I can't speak!"

The reason he had this response was because he had not seen what had been spoken to him. God says, "Don't say I am a youth," and then after communicating with Jeremiah a little more God asks an amazing question. "Jeremiah, what do you see?" Jeremiah answered, "I see a branch of an almond tree." Then God says, "You have seen accurately and now I will perform my Word" (see Jer. 1).

What is interesting is that when Jeremiah saw what God wanted him to see, God was able to begin His task through Jeremiah. One of the words used in God's response is, "I will *watch* over my word to perform it." That word *watch* speaks of time. It also means, "accelerate." When you see things beyond your limited vision and you experience an "optical fusion" moment with God, everything speeds up and you move in a new realm of time.

Your sight needs to be fused with God's sight to make one percept, so that you can see your future as He sees it. Allow God to fuse your natural eyes with your spiritual eyes so you can see things from a new and higher perspective. You just might be surprised at what you will see.

CHILD IN MAN—THE INNOCENT EYE

A child once wrote in a note to God: "Dear God, your book has a lot of zip to it. I like science fiction stories. Your reader, Jimmy."

Pablo Picasso wrote: "It takes a very long time to become young again."

Let's understand the child's eye. According to psychologist Richard Stone, in the book *Children*, a child does not read critically, particularly when he reads for enjoyment. A child's reading is not critical, and it involves a certain innocent acceptance of all that he finds in print. A child approaches with an absence of critical self-consciousness. A child yields a quality of the kind with which critical intellect is not directly concerned, and so there is the absence of metafiction—fiction that discusses, describes, or analyzes a work of fiction.[2]

There is a difference between childlikeness and childishness. David was childlike, but his enemy King Saul was childish. Saul was provoked by David's innocence, and yet David was able to destroy a huge enemy of Israel. How? The innocent eye. Once the eye is darkened by the knowledge (which means a person has

experienced it) of good and evil, innocence is removed. God created man and woman with innocent eyes, but look what happens
in their Garden:

> *"When the woman **saw** that the fruit of the tree was
> good for food and pleasing to the eyes"* (Genesis 3:6, empha-
> sis added)

Her eyes influenced her. Remember that God created them
with a will of their own and a keen perception. She saw that the
fruit was pleasing to the eyes. That was where it all began: the eyes.

Our love for the past is beyond *unhealthy*, because as it is written in the ancient manuscript, *"Where there is no vision, the people
perish"* (Prov. 29:18 KJV). Simply put: the person who lives
focused on the past begins to decay. This is the method in which
our dark enemy starves the imagination. The word for *perish* that
our great father Solomon used in this Scripture is *parah* which
means, "to decay." The word *decay* means "to decline in quality,
power, and vigor." It also means, "to decompose."

Spiritual decadence usually comes after a peak or culmination
of achievements, and as a result, luxurious self-indulgence
becomes the order of the day instead of daily sacrifice.

FAITH—THE UNKNOWN PLACE

When you hear God's voice and act upon it, you become
acquainted with the emotions and feelings that go along with it.
Yes, there are emotions. Most times when I've heard something,

whether an impression or a "knowing" deep inside, I also experience anxiety simply because I'm not quite sure. Strange but true.

I have found that when God speaks, a new kind of faith is released—I call it untried faith. This is simple to understand, and the Scriptures define it in the New Testament Book of James: "...*Faith without works is dead*" (James 2:20). So if your faith has not worked for you, it is dead. Once you have tried that faith, and it has worked, it is quite realistically "known" faith. You become familiar with it, and in fact, you use that faith to touch and help other people.

An example would be sickness and the struggle that you may have had with a certain infirmity. You pray and believe that it will go away, and during the course of prayer, it disappears. Now you are acquainted with this specific challenge, and you have the faith to deal with it. Been there—done that. However, when something unknown comes along (a challenge you've never encountered before) it requires a different level of faith that has not been tried, and has not yet worked for you.

I love to use the ridiculous example of Moses and the rock. He and the Israelites in the wilderness had run out of water, and things were getting heated up. God spoke to Moses, and told him to do something that he had *never done before*. Moses was not acquainted with receiving water from a rock, and he had his doubts. He was acquainted with God demanding that he do outrageous things. After all, he had brought a few million people out from the clutches of their oppressors and had done various miracles with his staff, such as parting the waters of the sea. But now he was challenged with something entirely different. God told Moses to strike at the rock, and if he did, water would come from the rock.

Already some were calling him crazy, as he slowly walked toward a solid rock and raised his staff. He paused, and then suddenly struck *with precision and determination* (see Exod. 17:1-7). Sure Moses was struggling with anxiety because he had never done this before, and in fact this miracle had never happened before, which means that a higher level of faith was required from Moses—an unknown faith that required effort, struggle, and persistence.

Have you ever noticed in your life that when you first do something that you're unacquainted with, you feel nervous, anxious, and (in most cases) petrified? However, once you've overcome the various struggles and succeed, the next time you are required to do something similar, you find that you have adjusted to the requirements. The once mysterious and unknown thing is now a little easier to handle.

Remember when you first drove a vehicle? It was exhilarating, frightening, and adventurous. But perhaps now, years later, you have acquainted yourself with your surroundings. No longer do you drive slowly, measuring sides of the vehicle with fear that you may hit the pavement. Now, you *jump in and drive with a brand new perception*—no faith required.

When I got married to Jane in 1978, we agreed to have a child almost immediately. A few months later, Jane was pregnant with our first child, Donné. When we left the hospital, we were so careful carrying her, afraid to bump the stroller and take the chance of disturbing her. We placed her into the car and drove about 25 miles an hour, going slowly over every bump, and frustrating the other drivers on the road.

Didn't they understand that we had a newborn baby in the car, and even the slightest bump would possibly damage her? Well, we learned the nimbleness of a child and adjusted our driving accordingly. When our second child, Jacquelyn, was born, the driving and carefulness was no longer an issue, as we had now become acquainted with this and drove her home at a normal speed.

Once you have *worked* your faith, and are no longer afraid to operate in that realm, it stops being a stressful and emotionally strenuous work. Instead, it becomes much easier and faster to accomplish because you are no longer struggling internally with doubt and fear but rather are inspired by experience and boldness.

After Moses struck the rock and saw the results, his work was over, and God required him to move to a higher level of faith—back to the unknown. You will never be satisfied with the known—never; that's why it's so exciting when God speaks to you because He draws you into the unknown.

In the story where Moses is leading the Israelites into their promise, another problem arises: No water. This time God spoke to Moses and said, "Speak to the rock and water will come...." Moses had not experienced speaking to the rock, and decided to go with what he was acquainted with. He struck the rock, thereby making his action displeasing to God (see Num. 20:1-13). Why? God told him to speak to the rock, which was a higher dimension of faith required from Moses. Moses, for whatever reason, chose to stay within his comfort zone and do what he thought best, thus misrepresenting God.

...without faith it is impossible to please Him...
(Hebrews 11:6).

It didn't take much faith on Moses' part to strike the rock because he had done it before. However, it required a faith that Moses was not acquainted with to speak to the rock. This would've pleased God.

The prophetic word is a light that shines in a dark place. It is God's word. So let God change your view of the problem you're facing. When your perception of the problem changes, everything else will change along with it. A change in your perception will change *you* completely.

That's what prayer is for. Prayer does not change things, prayer changes *you*, and *you* change things. When prayer changes you and your perception of your circumstance, you can easily overcome. That's the way it works. That's the prophetic word in action.

ENDNOTES

1. Abraham Heschel, quoted in Richard Kehl, *Breathing On Your Own* (Seattle, WA: Darling & Company, 2001).

2. Richard Stone, quoted in Valeria Manferto De Fabianis, ed., *Children* (Vercelli, Italy: White Star S.P.A., 2006).

Chapter 7

He's In Your World

THE supernatural light of the future can never be confined to an exclusive group or culture. It's not to be hidden within a church or any other religious institution. The lives of many throughout history exemplify God's intention to bless the nations, while stepping outside of the box that the religious system has created. Unfortunately, too many of today's spiritual leaders only recognize the importance of divine communication within the context of their own mission, and they fail to recognize its need to interface in a larger world that desperately needs illumination. Jesus said:

> Now no one after lighting a lamp covers it over with a container, or puts it under a bed; but he puts it on a lampstand, so that those who come in may see the light (Luke 8:16).

Those who accurately recognize and follow God in their generation are those who contribute toward making the world a better place for all humankind. God's occupation and infiltration in our world supersedes the mechanics of any religious system and carries an infinite depth of benefit for those who are brave enough to delve into His mysteries.

Today God is raising people up to become His voice to their world. It's important to understand that it's not necessary to call yourself a prophet, and at times, doing so could prevent you from impacting your culture, in whatever field that may be. God speaks to and through all of us, not just to those who are called to be prophets. Although everyone starts small, ultimately you have to look beyond the known to do something significant.

To effectively impact your world, you must think practically and be able to see the need for God's voice, not only in religious circles but also in the marketplace. The ancient manuscripts contain examples of prophets who received inspiration used to meet practical needs, assisting in many areas such as finances, healings, and economic change for the nation.

Here are just a few examples that would undoubtedly seem crazy to the average person.

- Isaac became prosperous after God told him to remain in his own land during a famine, rather than going to Egypt to get help. (See Genesis 26.)

- Jacob made a business deal with his conniving father-in-law, Laban, that would make him very wealthy. Laban agreed to give Jacob all of his speckled and spotted livestock in return for Jacob's 20 years of work

for him. While Jacob was tending to the balance of
Laban's livestock, he had a crazy idea inspired by
God—he stuck a carved staff into the ground before
the eyes of the mating cattle and what they produced
was strong speckled and spotted livestock, leaving
Laban with a weaker and lesser amount of cattle.
Jacob had more than enough to prosper. (See Genesis
30.)

Moses was shown a tree that, when placed in an
undrinkable water supply, purified the water for the
people to drink. (See Exodus 15.)

While Syria was making war against Israel, the
prophet Elisha, by means of his gift, heard the secret
strategies of the king of Syria, and shared the information with the king of Israel to assist him in win-
ning the war. (See Second Kings 6.)

Saul went to the prophet Samuel and received assis-
tance to find his father's donkeys. (See First Samuel 9-
10.)

A medical cure for a deadly growth was given to
Isaiah the prophet for a king who was dying. Isaiah
did something crazy, something that he heard in a
moment of inspiration—he placed a mixture of figs
on the dying king's growth. The king recovered
because of this crazy action. God will give you a

method to apply a divine principle. (See Isaiah 38:21.)

🌿 Jesus Christ sent Peter to the sea to fish for tax
money. The first fish he caught contained a coin
worth enough to pay the taxes for both of them. Peter
had to do what he was told to do by the living word—
Christ. It was crazy, yes, but Peter obeyed and was
rewarded. (See Matthew 17.)

There are many other examples of men whose valuable
insights benefited the people who received them. God's good
intention toward humankind has never changed. However, His
methods have changed. The method that He once used in the past
may not produce a miracle when repeated. There will only be
supernatural intervention when a method given by God is applied
in your world. He doesn't need to use old methods to apply old
principles. He has new methods for a generation and culture.
What worked for someone in another culture may not necessarily
work for you within your unique world and time.

We were created in His image, and I think it would be insult-
ing to misrepresent Him by being afraid to venture out as He does.
He is *innovative* which means "ahead of the times; advanced views
on the subject; producing something like nothing done or experienced or created before." You have an innovative and original
mind! Don't waste it because you're afraid of being called crazy!

Imagine what the angels thought when God did the craziest
thing ever—He took dust from the earth, breathed into it, and
spoke to it, and it became a living being. Wow. A *living being*
means "the state of continued existence." Are you living in a state
of *continued* existence or *stagnant* existence? If you're living in the

latter, then you are living in the same bracket as 90 percent of the population lives in—fear, boredom, anger, and resentment. The remaining 10 percent are living with freshness, passion, quick intelligence, and anticipation. How can they live like that? Because they love a challenge, which means that they are risk takers.

As you read previously, when you hear God, it's your last comfortable day on earth, but oh how tasty! If you are not living in a state of continued existence, then you are *not* hearing God, and you're afraid of losing ground in the field of comfort. Someone who is living in a state of stagnant existence has lost novelty. One of the things I've noticed about someone who gets inspired by a spiritual revelation and acts is that they have novelty. Novelty means that you carry an air of uniqueness and newness. In this day, where repetition and duplication have possessed most human beings in every walk of life, there is a need for uniqueness. When the novelty has worn off, a dangerous thief enters and steals one's predictive power. You are a novel occurrence.

RISK TAKERS, CARETAKERS, AND UNDERTAKERS

There are three types of people in the world—risk takers, caretakers, and undertakers. All of us fall into one of those three categories.

The *undertakers* have already dug your grave because they know you're not going to do it. They are the "naysayers" of this world who seek to bury what God is doing. They are the ones who say that the voice of God is not for today and that He no longer speaks to anyone.

The *caretakers* are always poking their noses into your business. They are trying to take care of things that no one ever asked them to take care of. They are the judges who declare what they believe is wrong in the church and the world. They determine who the false prophets are and what is heretical. They don't change the world; *they criticize the world*. They never take a risk. They live in the comfort of their own high towers.

Then there are the *risk takers*. They don't live in the world of the undertakers or the caretakers. They are pioneers and, sure, they may make mistakes, but they will make history too. Peter made his share of mistakes, but he walked on water while the other disciples were clinging to the boat. Peter had his eyes on Christ, and his sight was clear as he stepped out into the unknown. Yes, I know he sank for a moment, but he was the *only one* who actually walked on water. God loves risk takers!

I went to a church once and ran into some caretakers and undertakers. When I arrived, I immediately knew something was wrong. I went into the back of the auditorium where all of the leaders were sitting. They told me to sit down, and then proceeded to tell me that I could not prophesy about the future. I was only permitted to tell the things I sensed that had already happened. What they were really saying—I could talk about a person's past and their present, but they did not want me getting into that risky, mysterious place of predicting the future. I said, "What you are doing is taking away part of the revelation that exists in me." I told them that I would do my best to comply, but inside I felt angry and robbed.

Before I started speaking the next morning, I prayed, "God, please just let me speak to these people and get out of here without any conflict." I was just about to finish the service when God showed me a man who just lost his granddaughter and he was desperate. I knew I would be going against what I had been told to do, but I had to be faithful to God's word. So I said, "There's a gentleman here whose granddaughter has gone missing." The man I had seen came walking down the aisle with his wife. As I stood before them, I said, "I see that you have nineteen grandchildren. One of them is gone and her name is Janine." The man began to weep deeply at the accuracy of the word I had given. Then he grabbed my hands in desperation to hear what I had to say next about Janine, and in front of all of the people I said, "But I cannot tell you any more."

That night during the service I tried to handle things the same way; I revealed what I saw from the past and present but then stopped before revealing anything from the future. Being restricted proved too hard for me, and I decided to take a risk. I called out a lady and said, "God shows me that you have breast cancer and that you are going tomorrow for tests to find out how long you have left to live." She responded, verifying that what I was saying was correct.

I turned and looked at the religious leaders, knowing that I was really going to tick them off by what I was about to do. I turned back to the woman and said, "The report will come back and they will tell you that they can find no trace of the cancer!" The people started cheering and celebrating with the woman. She was given hope. "Hope deferred makes the heart sick…" (Prov. 13:12) and if the heart is sick, your body will be sick.

We have to give people hope. I'm not talking about false hope; I'm just saying I knew this was a sure word. I just knew it. The next morning I attended a breakfast with the leaders, and they began grilling me about the word I gave the woman with cancer. I told them I would stick to controlled speaking for the last night.

So, finally the evening arrives, and the meeting begins. I'm about to go to the piano when one of the doors at the back entrance of the church opens and a lady is standing there waving something. I had no idea who it was at the time, but as she started running down to the platform, I realized it was the same woman I spoke to about the cancer the night before. I knew it had to be some type of good news. She ran down and I saw that she had motor oil all over her arms. She was breathless as she cried out, "I've been trying to get here for awhile now but I had a flat tire and I had to change it myself." She said, "Take this paper! Look at it! It says that there's not a trace of cancer!" Thank God I took a risk.

God is the greatest risk taker of all time. He is the greatest adventurer in the world. He takes risks every day when He determines that He is going to use you and me to accomplish His work. Think about the risks He took throughout history—*His Story*.

The Israelites were pinned against the Red Sea, and there was no way out. Pharaoh and his army went after them in murderous fury. God intervened and spoke to Moses, telling him to do something crazy so they can get away (escape). He tells him to use his staff to strike the water—providing a dry path away from his pursuing enemies (see Exod. 14).

Then there's David and Goliath. Goliath, a seasoned soldier and trained killer, was confronted by God's choice—a freckled-face little shepherd kid with a slingshot. David does something really crazy; he uses a stone instead of a sword and gets the job done (see 1 Sam. 17).

Most commanders going into battle want to get as many infantry men as possible. But God cuts Gideon's army from 32,000 to 300. Then He instructs them to go and fight with the least of weapons—torches and pots (see Judg. 7). God loves to show up, show off, and take all the credit. He loves to prove human reasoning wrong.

Italian poet Antonio Porchia wrote, *"People who have their feet planted firmly on the ground often have difficulty getting their pants off."*

Novelist Anais Nin wrote, *"If I had not created my whole world, I would certainly have died in other people's."*

OCCUPATIONAL AND SITUATIONAL PERSPECTIVE

Occupational perspective is looking from the place that you plan to take control of and remaining there. People with an occupational perspective dare to see the potential that others do not see. This is a conscious attitude of those who are portentous. They are portentous of great change, expecting something momentous, and then they focus on that and not on the risk. They see loss as a step to a greater gain. Situational perspective is looking at what's around you and confining yourself to look from within your circumstances. People who see from a situational perspective are guided solely by what their natural eyes reveal to them.

Business men and women who maintain a situational perspective never rise above their circumstances and usually give up the thought of ever achieving great success. They choose to stay inside their self-limiting box. On the other hand, you have occupational businesspeople. They too have challenges all around them but are not afraid to take chances and step outside the borders to explore their opportunities. Their reputation is really not what they're concerned about. They are focused on success and doing what others are not doing. They don't often travel the beaten path.

Those with an occupational perspective pioneer new pathways in their chosen field. One of the last commands Jesus gave us before He left this earth was for us to occupy. He doesn't want us sitting around waiting for Him to come back; He wants us to keep busy and occupied.

God wants us to make a significant contribution in every part of our world, including business, politics, science, medicine, sports, music, entertainment, and of course, the family. Who does He plan to use? You! You have been chosen to impact at least one of these areas.

I've had the privilege of being used in many settings to deliver utterances given by God that have helped the lives of individuals all over the world and from all walks of life. I have also been entrusted to deliver significant messages to certain groups of people, nations, and even to the world. Today, we have the capability of monitoring the signs of the fulfillment of some of these predictions and have begun to do so through major news sources, using the Internet, television, and e-mail.

In 2005 I had the privilege of sharing a secret that God revealed to me about a discovery that would greatly assist our nation—the Big E.

THE BIG E

On May 22, 2005, in Dallas, Texas, precisely two months before the prophecy I delivered regarding Hurricane Katrina, I gave a prediction regarding a new energy source that would emerge. This is the transcript.

May 22, 2005 – Dallas, TX

"For the Spirit of God says, do you realize that there is a marked moment in time in the summer where there will be a divine transfer of masses of amounts of money? Keep your eye on the gold. Keep your eye on that one substance. Also keep your eyes open for you shall see things changing with petroleum. You shall see things changing with something new that will come forth. Invest into it. You'd better listen some of you investors; this is not petroleum. This is not oil. This is something else that is safer and God wants to share a secret tonight. Go and study it. I don't have the words. The Spirit of the Lord has hidden it from me. But He tells me there's something other than petroleum or gas or whatever you call it, oil, that's coming forth that's going to be used. Invest in it for it will bring some of you millions of dollars within a 14-month period says the Lord. It begins with an E. That's all I've got...the stock market is going to open up. NASDAQ is opening up."

Looking back, it's interesting to see that I gave this prediction regarding the new energy source and the rise of the economy prior to Hurricane Katrina leaving her trail of great destruction on the Gulf Coast of the United States. This storm, that destroyed 30 oil platforms and caused the closure of nine refineries, was said to be the costliest natural disaster in United States history.

Though I have given many predictions that have incited controversy, this one regarding the new energy source seems to have sparked a new interest, especially among investors. The secrets regarding this word from the Lord have continued to come like pieces of a puzzle, which can only be assembled correctly in proper timing.

Since the Big E has become a subject of great interest, let me show you just a few more pieces of this puzzle, in chronological order, along with a few possibly related articles that followed in the news. In so doing, you can see how my gift sometimes works regarding something that is about to take place or be discovered which may suggest national significance. All of these, of course, were given in verifiable public settings as I spoke in cities throughout the United States.

On September 3, 2005, in Whittier, California, I prophesied that this new energy will come from within the United States, and I saw that it would come from the garbage, the ground, the paper, and bugs eating things.

"There will be a source that they will have within this nation. It shall come from the garbage, it will come from the ground, it will come from paper, it will come from bugs eating a bunch of stuff. I'm seeing a bunch of bugs eating a bunch of stuff. God said this is going to be the craziest thing. They are going to say, 'Wow. This is being wasted. The creatures are eating what could be used to cause our engines to work and our vehicles to move.' I'm seeing this bunch of bugs eating this stuff and there it is, that's it right there. When this

happens, the United States shall rise above the wealth of the Middle East in terms of oil, and it shall take over."

September 9, 2005, in Portland, Oregon, I saw that it would come from the rocks and from the earth.

"They are saying, 'Oh, you said the oil and the economy shall be revived.' Are you looking to oil when I already have something else that I shall use from your rocks and from your earth? Do you realize that America is being forced to embark upon a new energy source? America has been forced to go as pioneers again and create a new form of energy. And it's already there, it's right under your feet. It's not coming from anywhere else. It's not coming from the Middle East. It's coming from the soil of this nation!"

On September 17, 2005, in Detroit, Michigan, I predicted that once the new energy source comes, it will provide enough to clear the deficit and that it would be related to a six-year period. I also saw a connection with Israel and hidden oil.

"...it shall take you from a trillion dollar deficit to no deficit whatsoever within a six-year period says the Spirit of God. And the Middle East shall say you still need oil. But America shall say no longer from you, for Israel 'Oh Israel what is hidden shall be revealed' says the Lord."

On December 31, 2005, in San Jose, California, I was shown the new source was related to something Albert Einstein was in the process of discovering, and that NASDAQ would rise to its highest place ever.

"...I will show My servants, the prophets, the places to invest and some shall say, 'this is an Einsteinian craze' but it shall come from something that Einstein was discovering and bringing forth, but before his time, therefore I had to remove him. This is the time where discovery shall bring a new source of energy and it shall start in this nation, says the Lord. Do not say, 'Einstein, what about God?' God said, I worked wonders but now some of the theories shall become fact and God said, it shall be so surprising that people shall say, 'what shall we do?' America—No deficit! America—No deficit!...

"NASDAQ, you have fallen. You have been raised up, and gone back down. But now it's time to rise to the highest place ever. Listen to the secrets of the Lord."

USA Today—NASDAQ at 5-year high as stocks rebound

Updated 3/29/2006 11:25 PM

By Matt Krantz

The tech-packed NASDAQ powered up 33.32 points, or 1.4%, to 2337.78 for its highest close in more than five years.[1]

USA Today—Gold price tops $700 an ounce as tensions rise

Updated 5/10/2006 1:29 PM ET

By John Waggoner

Gold soared above $700 an ounce Tuesday for the first time since 1980, propelled by rising international tensions and a falling dollar.[2]

CBS—Dow Tops 12,500 For First Time

New York, Dec. 27, 2006 (AP)

Wall Street surged higher Wednesday, hurtling the Dow Jones industrials past 12,500 for the first time as year-end bargain hunters picked up stocks across a variety of sectors.[3]

FOX News—Stocks Get Boost From Strong Economic Data

Friday, June 01, 2007

A government report showing a stronger-than-expected rise in new jobs in May got Friday's session to a strong start, sending the Dow industrials to an all-time high and the S&P 500 index to its highest in more than seven years. A gauge of U.S. manufacturing activity also rose, lending support.[4]

On September 10, 2006, in a Secrets gathering in Hollywood, California, I heard that though the oil will be plentiful, so it should not be a concern, we were to watch for the Big E.

"...You say, what about oil? Oil will be plentiful. We're not talking about oil. God said, watch the Big E."

FOX News—Gasoline Prices Won't Be as High This Summer as in 2006, Government Says

Tuesday, April 10, 2007

WASHINGTON — Motorists can expect higher pump prices in the months ahead, but gasoline will cost less on average than last summer and supplies will be plentiful, the government said on Tuesday.[5]

On September 16, 2006, in Loveland, Colorado, a clue regarding the timing of the Big E and other details were revealed.

> "...The other shall be the stepping down of a Prime Minister of the Lion of the Nation of Great Britain. For when he does this, says the Lord, it shall be a sign, not because he stepped down. A sign that something shall advance, something shall advance out of Great Britain. Something shall advance, says the Spirit of God, from the United States. And I will take them and I will make them to be one sound and one voice, a very unusual revival, a very unusual breakthrough shall take place, says the Lord. And there shall be an acceleration on the oil crisis and discoveries shall be made one after the other. And God said your energy crisis shall slowly come to an end for I am going to bring prosperity upon the Body of Christ and upon those who have waited and said, God, I want you to lay upon me that blessing that you promised through Daniel, that blessing that you promised through Joseph, the blessing that you promised through Isaiah, the blessing that you promised through the prophets of old. I'm standing at this day where the Kingdom of God is about to advance upon the earth."

FOX News—Britain PM Tony Blair Plans to Step Down

Thursday, May 10, 2007

By Paisley Dodds, AP writer

In government you carry each hope, each disillusion... Blair said last September, near the beginning of what has been a long, slow march toward an announcement Thursday that he will step down to allow for a party leadership contest that will likely end this summer.[6]

On December 8, 2006, in Portland, Oregon, I was given a prophecy that seemed to relate this with another great discovery and a matter in the field of medicine. A breakthrough was said to come the following May or June.

"The Spirit of God says, a very unusual matter regarding the field of medicine where they will not allow certain ideas regarding creativity, and once it happens there will be a breakthrough in the May or June of next year. But you see things, read things; do not listen to them. But I already sent out cures where some great, great discovery shall take place, a neurological discovery that will bring those with certain disorders into a place of healing. Look to the autistic children. For God says, autistic children, if they survive and they come out of it, and the discovery is made, shall be the geniuses of the world."

ABC—Florida Man Invents Machine To Cure Cancer

POSTED: 11:49 am EST February 27, 2007

SANIBEL ISLAND, Fla. – A Florida man with no medical training has invented a machine that he believes may lead to a cure for cancer.

John Kanzius, who turns 63 on March 1, is a former broadcast executive from Pennsylvania who wondered if his background in physics and radio could come in handy in treating the disease from which he suffers himself.

Inside his Sanibel Island garage, Kanzius invented a machine he believes sits on the brink of a major medical breakthrough.[7]

Note: Also see news link below the prediction for May 20, 2007, which was posted on ABC-WPBF Website May 24, 2007.

On December 31, 2006, in San Jose, California, I was given a prophecy to watch the minerals and that a tree would be the sign of the Big E. I also predicted there was a link related to a discovery in a vehicle in Michigan.

"Men and women who have longed to go into the marketplace, fear not, do not fear anymore; the marketplace has been opened up says the Lord of Hosts. NASDAQ, NASDAQ you have now risen to a place where you are prideful, but God says this is a sign, for the economy of this nation shall rise above and shall begin to dictate to the nations of the earth. The strength of the dollar shall come because of the strength of the spiritual life in this nation. Watch me take possession of Wall Street says the Spirit of the Lord. Watch the minerals says the Spirit of God for even in this next year you shall see a great rising, but do not fear. Look to the tree, for the tree is a sign of that which will come with the "E" says

the Spirit of the Lord. A new source of energy is now rapidly coming to pass...

The molecule as an "E," a new source of energy that we have spoken of, is now to be unfolded, a discovery in a vehicle from Michigan; they shall say it was so simple."

On February 2, 2007, in Seattle, Washington, I prophesied more indicating it was not simply ethanol, as some had assumed.

"A new source of energy shall suddenly emerge from the hollow, from nothing, from junk. Do not say it is ethanol. I'm about to surprise you and show this nation that the claws of those that have stood in the Middle East and in South America that have said we will hold onto them, God says I will shake them off you."

On February 3, 2007, in Seattle, Washington, I predicted something insignificant will become the greatest source of energy for the world. I also saw something major happening in south Florida.

"Something significant is going to happen in this nation by a very insignificant event. God's going to take of your dust, He's going to take of your trash, He's going to take of your soil, He's going to take of your bugs something insignificant and make it the greatest source of energy for the world. There will be a major move of the Spirit in south Florida.

On February 18, 2007, in Toledo, Ohio, another piece of the puzzle was revealed to me. I saw that this great discovery was also somehow related to the work of Einstein.

"I can stand before somebody that's about to be the President of the United States and say don't worry about the oil crisis because God told me there's going to be a new source of energy. It's called the Big E. What's the Big E? We know about ethanol. God says, no there's something else which came from Einstein that you're going to find out and this nation will tell the Middle East you can take your oil and shove it because God says I've got something new I'm going to reveal to you.

On April 29, 2007, in Reseda, California, I saw more regarding its timing.

"For God says, even as you have heard and learned that a new source of energy is coming, many have said, ethanol, ethanol, but God said, watch what I do. I will take from nothing and make something and in the month of May there will be favorable exchanges and they will make announcements but God said, rejoice, rejoice children of the King for in this month I have set aside a window of opportunity as never before."

On May 4, 2007, in Orlando, Florida, I received a prediction regarding a sign that would come, of a find of great wealth in the sea.

"The Spirit of God says, Do not take lightly what was spoken about concerning the sea. For there is something that is taking place in the sea. Vengeance is in the sea. A battlefield under the waters, why? Because of the great wealth that shall come from the waters deep down. No not from the moon, no not from another planet, not yet; but God said from the sea

that will bring a healing. Hence you will see the battle in the sea. The corruption shall be exposed. For even as Elijah went to the house of the woman at Zarephath. Oil, sticks, dirt, all of these components now to bring an abundance to the United States of America. Sticks, dirt, oil, water and the amalgamation and God says it shall be something that has never, ever happened before. And this nation shall speak of water; oil, dirt, and the amalgamation shall bring an energy. Therefore look to the sign of the battlefield in the waters."

On May 5, 2007, in Orlando, Florida, more came about the wealth in the sea, a link to the story of Simon Peter going to find the coin in the fish's mouth, and some details I saw of an emblem.

"I delight in the prosperity of My people. As I told Simon Peter, find the fish, for the wealth is in the fish. They will fight but there is great wealth, great energy not yet detected which I will blind them to. For I will only allow My Nation that will honor Me to have this first fruits. You have given therefore you shall be honored says the Lord. I see an emblem of the octopus. It has a star, it has something underneath it and this is an organization that shall arise. Fear not, for as I told you I laugh at those who would strike at this Nation."

FOX News—Deep-Sea Explorers Discover Possible Richest Shipwreck Treasure in History

May 18, 2007

Deep-sea explorers said Friday they have hauled up what could be the richest sunken treasure ever discovered: hundreds of thousands of colonial-era silver and gold coins worth an estimated $500 million from a shipwreck in the Atlantic Ocean.[8]

FOX News—Spain Probes Treasure Hunters Sunday

Sunday, May 20, 2007

The Spanish government is investigating if a crime was committed by a U.S. company that said it had found $500 million worth of coins in an Atlantic Ocean shipwreck, according to Sunday news reports.

Odyssey Marine Exploration, based in Tampa, Fla., revealed on Friday they had found hundreds of thousands of colonial-era silver and gold coins in the wreck, but didn't release details about the ship or the wreck site, citing security concerns.[9]

FOX News—Shipwreck Treasure Brings Claims, Rumors

Monday, May 21, 2007

Deep-sea explorers who found what could be the richest-ever shipwreck treasure said Monday that the reaction to their discovery has overwhelmed them. Meanwhile, claims on the loot started coming in even as they were exploring new waters— television and movie deals.

Odyssey Marine Exploration on Friday announced 'the recovery of more than 500,000 Colonial-era silver and gold coins possibly worth $500 million. The exploration company from Tampa has withheld details about the ship-wreck, where it was found or even what kind of coins they had hauled back.

"We are overwhelmed by the worldwide interest in this project, and it reinforces our belief that shipwreck exploration hits a nerve with the public. I wasn't prepared for the response," Odyssey co-founder Greg Stemm said.[10]

On May 20, 2007, in San Jose, California, I was shown that the find of great wealth in the seas would be a sign regarding the new energy source.

"For the Spirit of God says watch in this month the discoveries that this prophet prophesied about. I spoke about treasures that will come to this Nation and will come from sources least expected. I spoke about a silver coin in the fish's mouth. Do you understand that even now as there has been a discovery of these coins, this is nothing. For this nation there will be a discovery within the sea that shall cause a war and people will say we must war for this but it will be short lived. I will not allow them to take from this nation again because it's in your waters. I give this to you says the Spirit of God. They will say this has never ever happened before. The Spirit said, now watch the seas. Watch the wealth that comes as a sign."

ABC—Florida Man Invents Machine To Turn Water Into Fire

Thursday, May 24, 2007

SANIBEL ISLAND, Fla. — A Florida man may have accidentally invented a machine that could solve the gasoline and energy crisis plaguing the U.S.[11]

FOX News—Colombia Fights U.S. Diver for Treasure

Sunday, June 03, 2007

By Joshua Goodman

BOGOTA, Colombia — The Spanish galleon, San Jose, was trying to outrun a fleet of British warships off Colombia's coast on June 8, 1708, when a mysterious explosion sent it to the bottom of the sea with gold, silver and emeralds now valued at more than $2 billion.

"Without a doubt the San Jose is the Holy Grail of treasure shipwrecks," said Robert Cembrola, director of the Naval War College Museum in Newport, R.I."[12]

On June 16, 2007, in San Jose, California, I was given the most recent word, as of the date of the completion of this book, regarding the Big E. God showed me there would be five new sources. Also that the Pacific, the West Coast, would also share in a great discovery regarding energy. It will be linked to something they discover in the land, air, sea, dolphin, whale, and octopus. And more…

> "…God says there is a mass treasure that's about to be uncovered. God said, My people will get it. My people will take it. For the forces that have hidden and endeavored to hide what is about to be uncovered, they have been annihilated. They have been dreadfully secured. And now even as I have promised, through these next few months, one thing after the other will be uncovered. Down in Florida it began, but on the Pacific, the West Coast, there is also great discovery. You will not have to struggle for the breakthrough that is

coming to you. The struggle is over. You're going over, you're not going under says the Lord of hosts.

"*There is a miraculous thing that is about to be uncovered. For even in the stepping down of Tony Blair, this is a sign. A good man, a man that I have used as a friend to this nation. But God says there will be a sign with the great E. There will be rapidity, and there will be acceleration so that America will suddenly have five new sources of energy. There will be five, not one, but five. Why would anybody be interested? For let the prophets prophesy. There will be five sources of energy. And they will say, what will we do now? We have so many sources!*

"*Shall we create and design an engine in this way? And shall we design a plane in this way? And we shall not use this but we shall use another. And what about the air? What is in the air? What is in the sea? What is in the land? What is in the air? What is in the dolphin and the whale and the octopus? Listen, God says, America, get ready to stand upright again. I will cause my Church to prosper first for I will give the pattern to you. For this day I have said, I will secure it until I find a righteous man who will take it and say 'I have patented it for the Kingdom of God, and it shall be given for God's work and God's work shall accelerate' says the Lord.*"

As you can see, this revelation regarding the new energy source did not come to me all at once. Even now, as I write, it is still unfolding. Piece by piece, the picture is coming together. What I do know is God spoke to me and said He will bless the economy of this great nation and from it will bring forth new energy sources. Since these first predictions, we have seen signs of its beginnings. Although I have not yet been given the complete picture of this new energy source, we have already received reports of eager investors who have made profitable investments based on their own research of these prophecies.

I know it may sound crazy to you, but I'm hearing God!

You may ask, why would God share something about the economy of the United States? In Chapter 4, I established the fact that prophets were called to be a blessing to the nations. A blessing invokes divine favor and protection. God's intentions are to strengthen the economy of nations and the marketplace, but just as has always been the case, someone must go into those places and become the voice of God.

JOSEPH

Joseph was empowered to help guide Egypt through a famine that he saw coming upon the land through a dream from God. Though he is remembered best for the story of his famous coat of many colors and his skillful God-given ability to interpret dreams, Joseph suffered a harsh betrayal at the hands of his own brothers while on his path to fulfilling his destiny. As a young man, Joseph dreamed of greatness. His brothers were enraged with jealousy and considered murdering him, but decided instead to sell him away into slavery. Through this tragic experience, Joseph wound up in an Egyptian prison, and there his journey began.

Prisoners and even the royalty of Egypt recognized Joseph's gift as he gave spiritual insight to those around him. Soon he was favored and released from the prison to be promoted to a position in the government. He would provide strategic counsel and insight regarding Pharaoh's dreams and the economy of Egypt. The ancient manuscripts tell us that Pharaoh favored Joseph so much that he made him ruler over all of the land of Egypt. He gave him one of his own rings, expensive clothing, a gold chain around his neck, and a special chariot so he would be honored as he rode through the land. (See Genesis 41.)

Joseph's brothers came to Egypt looking for help during the famine, and though they never expected to see him again, they found themselves at the mercy of the brother they had betrayed. Joseph forgave his brothers and restoration took place within their family. The place Joseph now ruled and occupied would become the source of provision to all his people.

God wanted a voice in Egypt. He didn't send a man who thought he had all the answers. He sent a man who found his way step by step into the place where he was destined to help his fellow prisoners, the royalty of Egypt, and eventually his own family and people. Despite all that Joseph had suffered, he had an occupational perspective that took him to the top, where he had influence over all of Egypt and its economy.

When Joseph's brothers sold him into slavery, they actually sold the voice that would one day rescue them from famine. They soon went from being kings to slaves. There are consequences when we lose value of what God actually gave for our benefit. Similarly, when you do not recognize the value of hearing Him in your life, you will go from reigning to being ruled over. Therefore, we must never "sell" the prophetic voice, for it is more desperately needed today than it was in ancient times. Joseph went to the top, not simply because he was destined to be great, but because he understood the value of hearing God from a young age. *He went to bed a prisoner and woke up a prime minister.* His brothers couldn't hold him back, and no one can hold you back, when you highly esteem His voice in your life and choose to follow Him wherever that may lead.

Joseph not only influenced the economies of his world, but he was also an instrument for restoration. He used his influence to save the lives of his family. Once we fulfill our own destiny, we can then bring others to the place we have occupied.

DANIEL

Daniel was a prophet who God used to infiltrate the Kingdom of Babylon. However, he wasn't sent to fight or prophesy against the culture. Through the demonstration of his gift and favor, Daniel became a ruler in Babylon. His story began nearly a century after the kingdom of Israel had come to an end at the hands of the Assyrians. Nebuchadnezzar deported the Jews immediately after his victory over the Egyptians at the second battle of Carchemish.

In the fourth year of the reign of Jehoiakim (606 b.c.), Daniel and three of his peers, Shadrach, Meshack, and Abednego, were carried off to Babylon along with some of the vessels of the temple. Daniel and his three Jewish friends were carefully tested and chosen for their intellect and favored appearance, to be trained as Chaldeans and to advise the Babylonian court.

Daniel was chosen to enter into the service of the king of Babylon. He was then assigned the Chaldean name of

Belteshazzar, which means "Bel protect the king." However, through it all, Daniel and his three friends remained fervently devoted to their Jewish spiritual identity. Eventually Daniel had to answer for his apparent divided interest to the Babylonian court.

Daniel's training in Babylon (see Dan. 1:4) was allowed by God, not to corrupt him, but to prepare him for service to the empire. Some would call this compromise, but actually he was carefully being prepared to become the voice of God to a kingdom that desperately needed His direction. Daniel set himself apart during his training period for his strong commitment to God and gained favor with those who were over him.

After three years of intense training in Babylon, Daniel was known for his proficiency in the pagan wisdom of his day. Soon he was known for his pure prophetic gift, and he showed great skill in the interpretation of dreams. As Daniel gained favor and demonstrated his gift, he also rose to the rank of governor of the province of Babylon and became chief of the governors over all the wise men. Daniel was given this favor after displaying exemplary gifting in counsel to the king, over all the magicians, astrologers, sorcerers, and Chaldeans in Babylon. In doing so, he actually saved all of their lives (see Dan. 1-2).

Daniel was another one who occupied the territory he was sent to possess. Can you imagine? Daniel was a prophet of God in Babylon! What would a modern-day Daniel look like? What about the rejection and accusations that would come from the religious rulers who had no way of controlling him? He learned the language of the Babylonian kingdom and excelled, and it was said that he was found to be ten times better than all of the rest, while remaining committed to one God.

Daniel did not fight the culture or the practices found within the Babylonian kingdom. He had an occupational perspective and he occupied that territory. You don't need to separate yourself from your culture. You should excel beyond others who have no true source of illumination and inspiration and become the voice of God to them.

ETERNITY IN YOUR DNA

The great Solomon penned this powerful statement, "...[God] *has put eternity in their hearts...*" (Eccles. 3:11). Eternity flows from your blood and is locked in your DNA. In other words, humanity will never be satisfied until it connects with something eternal. Eternity inside of you is the past, the present, and the future all in one. You are in time and space and what you are looking for has *already happened*. What you are praying for has *already been answered*. Your future is here and you look much better than you do right now!

Each of us live our lives within the restrictions of our time-and-space world. All of us have experienced what appears to be the speeding up and slowing down of time. Have you ever noticed that when you are on vacation that time seems to just fly by? You are having so much fun, and before you know it, your vacation is over. On the contrary, the reverse happens when you are in a tedious and unwanted moment. When you are on a job that you hate, it appears that time seems to just drag by. You sit at your desk watching the slow ticking of the clock, and it seems like the day will never end.

Is it possible to delay or speed-up time?

Albert Einstein thought it was possible. One of Einstein's greatest insights was realizing that time is relative. It speeds up or slows down depending on how fast one thing is moving relative to something else. He called the slowing of time due to motion *time dilation*. It is interesting how the motion of our life seems to affect the advance of time.

Einstein concluded toward the end of his life that the past, present, and future all exist simultaneously. In his famous book, *Relativity*, Einstein penned these words:

> Since there exists in this four dimensional structure [space-time] no longer any sections which represent "now" objectively, the concepts of happening and becoming are indeed not completely suspended, but yet complicated. It appears therefore more natural to think of physical reality as a four dimensional existence, instead of, as hitherto, the evolution of a three dimensional existence.[13]

Einstein's belief in an undivided solid reality was clear to him, so much so that he completely rejected the separation we experience as the moment of now. He believed there is no true division between past and future, but that there is rather a single existence. His most descriptive testimony to this faith came when his lifelong friend Besso died. Einstein wrote a letter to Besso's family, saying that although Besso had preceded him in death it was of no consequence, "*...for us physicists believe the separation between past, present, and future is only an illusion, although a convincing one.*"[14]

The Reward

My journey has not been easy. Sometimes the adversity blinds and keeps a prophet from seeing the rewards. There was a time when I was so frustrated, and it seemed as if there was more persecution than I could endure. I got angry with God. I went into a room and locked the door and said, "OK, I'm sick of this. What reward is there? Where is the reward you promised?"

I traveled a lot, especially in the early days, and I was away from my family often. Sometimes it was very difficult for me to leave them at home. There was a point when I was getting angry about all the traveling. I just didn't want to travel any more. I was tired and wanted to just give up for a while.

During that season, I remember when I was going to San Francisco, and I hated to say goodbye. I didn't like telling my children I was going to do church work because I didn't want them to relate my absence to church. So I would always say I was going to work, like other people do. As I was preparing to leave for that trip, my second daughter, Jacquelyn, had this look on her face that I can't really describe. It was as if she couldn't believe that I was leaving again. I had made a commitment, and knew that I had no choice.

While I was at the airport, waiting for the departure, I was angry. I wanted to go home. Then I heard God's voice invade my anger. I heard God say, "I'm sending you to San Francisco for a reason." I responded rather despondently, "God find somebody else, please. I cannot stand seeing that look on my child's face anymore. I have to be home now."

I waited at the airport for a long time. Then I heard them calling the San Francisco flight. I just sat there, looking straight ahead. Finally, I heard them call my name a few times, but I continued to sit there. Eventually the flight took off without me, and I was actually happy.

I stood up to leave when a lady approached me and said, "Hello Mr. Clement!" I wasn't feeling very cordial, but I said hello to her anyway. She then said, "I want to tell you something. You were in Pittsburgh two years ago, and you called me out of the crowd and said, 'You're crying for your daughter.'" I didn't remember the situation she was describing. She went on to say that when her daughter was 16 years of age she had left home. She had been crying out to God for her daughter to come back home. She said, "You told me that my daughter was in the Florida Keys, and she'd be back in two days. Two days later, my daughter came back after being away for months, while the police were looking for her. My daughter ran into my arms sobbing and tender toward us. We were reunited just because you came to our city."

I was very touched and thanked her for reminding me of this story. I decided to stay at the airport and get on the next flight to San Francisco, yet still with a heavy heart. There were over 2,000 people in the meeting that night, and I knew I was doing what I was supposed to be doing. In the middle of my speaking, I heard God tell me to go to the back of the building.

I stopped what I was doing and walked to the back of the room. It was a huge place and in the very last row there was a young man sitting there and he was shaking. God said, "That's the one." I told the young man to stand up and he said no. I knew this man was scared of religion. I found out later that someone had told him to come because a prophet was going to be there. He took a risk by coming because he was scared of religion, but wanted to see what a prophet had to say. I told him to come with me up to the platform; that this was going to be his night.

I walked him to the front and told him that God revealed to me that he had AIDS and that the doctors had told him that he had three months to live. He fell to his knees weeping. I didn't speak about his sin or lay any guilt on him. I said, "God said you're going to stand before tens of thousands of gay people and tell them how God came into your life and touched you!" It was such a beautiful moment. He hugged me, crying, and went back to his seat. I finished my work and went home to my family, very pleased with what God had done through me in San Francisco.

I didn't hear anything more about this young man and didn't know what happened to him after that meeting. Two or three years later, I was in San Diego, and my host said to me, "Kim, before you actually take the stage, would you allow me to bring a guest on just to sing a song?" I told him that would be fine and that I didn't mind.

So I sat down and they brought a young man out to sing. I had no idea who he was. Before he sang, he began to tell me that two and a half years ago, doctors had told him that he had three months to live. At the invitation of a friend, he had reluctantly gone to a church in Oakland, California. He said that he went to that meeting with no hope, as the doctors had given up on him. He went on to say that he was not a church person and was afraid the church would condemn him.

He said, "This man was on the platform preaching, when he stopped his message, came right to the back row of the building where I was sitting, and pointed at me. He told me that I would live to make a declaration to tens of thousands of gay people. The man who spoke into my life that day was Kim Clement."

He said, "Mr. Clement, I have a song to sing to you, but before I sing I want to tell you that I was just in Romania where I spoke at a gay convention with tens of thousands of gays in attendance. When my turn came, they thought I was going to propagate the rights of gays, but I asked them if I could sing them a song. They all cheered and I went on to sing about Jesus and then said, 'I've only got two minutes left and I want to tell you what Jesus did for me and what he can do for you.' The response was astonishing and many stood there receiving the love and acceptance of Jesus Christ."

He turned to me and said, "You know why all of this happened for me? It happened because you came to San Francisco, and you touched my life." I sat there deeply moved by this man's story and so thankful to God that I decided to get on the plane that day to San Francisco.

Miraculously, that man lived another seven years without a trace of sickness. He never deteriorated and, in fact, he got healthier. Sadly, he passed away eight years later after living with a disease that should have taken him within months.

The day before he died, he called me and said, "I want to thank you for being the father that I never had. For a moment you gave up being a father to become a father to me." I cannot explain to you the feeling I had when I heard those words. It made me weep. It was the most wonderful feeling to have touched a life and then to have that life give back so much more.

That's the reward God had promised me. God had said to me, "I'll be a father to your children, if you go and be a father to the fatherless." That man influenced thousands of lives because I took that step, got on the plane, and threw out my desire out to be in a comfortable place, to be in my own house with my own family.

This is the reward.

ENDNOTES

1. Matt Krantz, "NASDAQ at 5-year high as stocks rebound," *USA Today*, 29 March 2006, www.usatoday.com/money/markets/us/2006-03-29-stocks-wed_x.htm.

2. John Waggoner, "Gold price tops $700 an ounce as tensions rise," *USA Today*, 9 May 2006, http://www.usatoday.com/money/markets/2006-05-09-gold_x.htm.

3. "Dow Tops 12,500 For First Time," *CBS*, 27 December 2006, http://www.cbsnews.com/stories/2006/12/27/business/main2303286.shtml.

4. "Stocks Get Boost From Strong Economic Data," *FOX News*, 1 June 2007, http://www.foxnews.com/story/0,2933,277012,00.html.

5. "Gasoline Prices Won't Be as High This Summer as in 2006, Government Says," *FOX News*, 10 April 2007, http://www.foxnews.com/story/0,2933,265128,00.html.

6. Paisley Dodds, "Britain PM Tony Blair Plans to Step Down," *FOX News*, 10 May 2007, http://www.foxnews.com/wires/2007May10/0,4670,FarewelltoBlair,00.html.

7. "Florida Man Invents Machine To Cure Cancer," *ABC*, 27 February 2007, http://www.wpbf.com/health/11125485/detail.html.

8. "Deep-Sea Explorers Discover Possible Richest Shipwreck Treasure in History," *FOX News*, 18 May 2007, http://www.foxnews.com/story/0,2933,273512,00.html.

9. "Spain Probes Treasure Hunters Sunday," *FOX News*, 20 May 2007, http://www.foxnews.com/wires/2007May20/ 0,4670,TreasureShipSpain,00.html.

10. "Shipwreck Treasure Brings Claims, Rumors," *FOX News*, 21 May 2007, http://www.foxnews.com/wires/2007May21/ 0,4670,TreasureShip,00.html.

11. "Florida Man Invents Machine To Turn Water Into Fire," *ABC*, 24 May 2007, http://www.wpbf.com/news/13383827/ detail.html.

12. Joshua Goodman, "Colombia Fights U.S. Diver for Treasure," *FOX News*, 3 June 2007, http://www.foxnews. com/wires/2007Jun03/0,4670,ColombiaSunkenFortune,00.html.

13. Albert Einstein, quoted in "Albert Einstein and the Fabric of Time," *Timelessness*, http://everythingforever.com/ einstein.htm.

14. *Ibid.*

Chapter 8

I Found Someone to Talk To

FOR too long, Christians have focused so much of their attention on trivial matters like what we should be wearing and the use of profanities, that their influence on society has become completely irrelevant. Their personal "convictions" make them somehow feel better. The fact is, it is not our holiness that makes anyone listen to us, but the relevance of the message and how they can relate to it in their daily lives. Who can relate to someone who is portraying so much holiness, that they have no earthly relevance?

I'm not saying that the use of profanity, violence, or sexual immorality is acceptable, but for some reason religion has made us believe that in displaying "holy" characteristics we will impress the unbeliever and win a soul.

However, what really matters to humanity? And why is religion completely and utterly failing to effect society?

Culture is the prevailing value system of a group of people; as it is expressed through politics, education, arts, athletics, etc. It comes from the Latin word *cultus* which means worship. *Cult* is to worship your beliefs. When we become advocates of a creed, something dies. We do not believe God, we only believe our beliefs about God.

The church historically and repeatedly talks about Christ's eternal state of existence but barely discusses His walk on earth. According to the ancient manuscripts, He was a whole man with intellect and feelings, and He experienced every human feeling we do. For a minute, let's forget the sin factor and look at human nature. Contrary to what many people believe, human nature is *not* evil. God created us as human beings with a body, mind, *and* spirit. The spirit is able to receive the divine nature from God, and the effect on our human nature varies. Our human nature, if controlled by sin, will be offended by God's nature, and this will cause friction, resistance, and conflict. Guilt, constantly driving our decisions will bring more chaos and disaster into our environment, and the results are evident in our world today.

Everything that we need today, not only to survive, but also succeed, Jesus needed as a man. He needed affirmation. He asked His disciples, "Who do men say that I, the Son of Man am?" They answered him correctly and gave him the latest scoop from the *Jerusalem Gazette. "Some say John the Baptist, some Elijah, and others Jeremiah or one of the prophets"* (see Matt. 16:13-20). Wow.

He was basically associated with one of the past prophets who was no longer on the earth. Christ had His own identity and His own personality, and did not need to be a prophet reincarnate. He was fresh, new, challenging, alive, compassionate, compelling, humble, powerful, charismatic, tender, brave, and had a powerfully irresistible effect on every human being who came into contact with Him. He was not going to accept a mold from the past. He did need affirmation though, and this is *not* a weakness, but proof that He was a human being with needs that humans have.

He proceeded to say, "Who do *you* say that I am?" His close disciple, a man with unusual braveness but usually swayed by involuntary impulses, suddenly stepped forward and made his declaration, something that could've cost him his life in the days of ancient religious law: "You are the Christ, the son of the Living God." Jesus, obviously touched by this statement, informed Peter that he had not heard this from any man, but from His Father in Heaven. God spoke out of a Palestinian Jewish larynx, and did not need any other phenomena to further his influence.

The following passage from the book, *The Jesus I Never Knew*, by Philip Yancey is such a beautiful piece to me.

> Each one relates to Jesus on his own terms, and in his own culture and within his own circumstances. The Italian movie *La Dolce Vita* opens with a shot of a helicopter ferrying a giant statue of Jesus to Rome. Arms outstretched, Jesus hangs in a sling, and as the helicopter passes over the landscape, people begin to recognize him. "Hey, it's Jesus!" shouts one old farmer, hopping off his tractor to race across the field. Nearer Rome, bikini-clad girls sunbathing around a swimming pool wave a friendly greeting, and the helicopter pilot swoops in for a closer look. Silent, with an almost doleful expression on his face, the concrete Jesus hovers incongruously above the modern world.

> How would I have responded to this man? Would I have invited him over for dinner, like Zacchaeus? Turned away in sadness, like the rich young ruler? Betrayed him, like Judas and Peter?

The more I study Jesus, the more difficult it becomes to categorize him. He said little about the Roman occupation, [the main topic of conversation among his countrymen], and yet took up a whip to drive petty profiteers from the Jewish temple. He urged obedience to the Mosaic Law while acquiring the reputation of a lawbreaker. He could be moved by sympathy for a stranger, yet turn on his best friend with the vicious rebuke, "Get behind me, Satan!" He had uncompromising views on rich men and loose women, yet both types enjoyed his company. One day, miracles seemed to flow out of Jesus; the next day his power was blocked by people's lack of faith. One day he talked in detail of the Second Coming; another, he knew neither the day nor hour. He fled from being arrested at one point and marched boldly toward it at another. He spoke eloquently about peacemaking, and then told his disciples to carry swords. His extravagant claims about himself kept him at the center of controversy, but when he did something truly miraculous he tended to hush it up."[1]

HOLLYWOOD

God told me that I was to go to Hollywood and build a work that would be a lighthouse to the lost. I realized that once my feet were committed to that soil, I would have to face the fact that the power of the media and the obvious presence of profanity, violence, fornication, etc., would offend me and try to stop me from "social infiltration." I further realized that I would be ineffective if I was "poisoned" by their sin because of this offense.

Since making the move, my moral standards have not been affected by their lifestyle. In fact, the mess I see them in drives me to a greater desire to be a voice, because I see the pathetic waste around them and feel compassion. Standing from the outside, separated on some religious island shouting at them will not save them. Jesus Christ never did that, why should I? He walked with them, had dinner with the sinner, allowed a women to touch his feet, did miracles in the presence of iniquity, and yet He never bowed to their standard of morality. He brought them to His state of existence—freedom.

Jesus wept at Lazarus' tomb, not because of the unbeliever, but because of the unbelief in the believer! When He was angered, it was not because of the sin of the sinners, but because of the sinful control of the Pharisees. Somehow, we have turned things around.

Like Jesus, Paul never stood on an island and shouted the odds about sin; rather, he engaged people in the battle of ideas and then presented the Truth to them while standing among them. The island Paul landed on came about because of a shipwreck. While on the island a snake bit him, and in the presence of the "heathen" Paul became a voice, because the snake's venom did not affect him.

Paul could clearly hear God in the most tempestuous times. He was barely affected by his circumstances and could steer an entire ship out of a deadly storm by simply obeying the voice he heard. Crazy? The story is told in the Scriptures in Acts 27:19-44. Paul did not only *hear* God, he also *acted* on what he heard, and in so doing, became God's voice by commanding, persuading, teaching, and demonstrating. He used his common sense at times and at other times, behaved as if he had lost his senses. He could stand before kings and prisoners alike and still communicate the exact same thing that he had heard. When in a desperate situation, he appealed to Caesar based on his Roman citizenship.

When you hear God, you have to go with what you were given, because (out of my experience) very little information is given most of the time. God has given you a spiritual ability to follow as He leads you, starting with a simple instruction. You have to make adjustments in order to "work it out."

As I've said before, while the church was measuring the length of skirts and the length of hair, scientists were discovering a greater means of transport; Bill Gates was gazing into the mystical ball of Microsoft, and women were legislating abortion, removing the rights of the unborn. The short skirts did lengthen, but it did not stop the adultery; the long hair did shorten, but it did not stop the rebellion; and millions of babies have died and billions of dollars have supplied the wrong people with power.

The church is supposed to be a family, a community, but instead it has become an organization that has separated itself— offering membership instead of relationship, demanding givers instead of forgivers, and piously rejecting defective souls while embracing the cream of the crop—or the, "cream of the crap," as I've been known to say.

The church, as we know it, has been abolished because the creeds of man and the theology of the pompous have clothed Jesus and tamed the Lion of Judah to the point of unrecognizable proportions. The world wants God, but they don't recognize the Jesus that religion has presented. They want that holy, simple Man whose day ended with dust on His feet, stains and spit on His robe, and tears in His hands.

They want the Man whose society included an immoral woman who was known for her serial marriages, a friend in a tomb, a young boy who provided some fish for a meal, a rich young ruler who walked away sad, little children surrounding Him, a Roman centurion begging for his paralyzed servant, a Jewish leader questioning His claims, a multitude praising Him as Messiah and then screaming for His crucifixion, a Judas who betrayed Him, a close friend who denied Him, and His night—His dark night not quite ending until He turned to a thief on a cross and offered to be His companion as he entered into paradise.

Somehow we lost something on the way, and my dream and my prayer is that we recapture the real Jesus and by our love and tolerance; present Him to the world.

Hole in the Roof

Author Philip Yancey wrote so eloquently about the experience of the paralytic and his four friends (see Mark 2:1-12):

> A man, who had spent his whole life horizontal, would have one moment of vertical fame, when he talked four friends into digging up a roof and lowering him through the hole. A hole in the roof is hardly the way to enter a house.

> Jesus was beneath him ministering and suddenly dust was flying, bits of straw and clay were falling on the guests, noise and chaos interrupted the meeting. The crowd whose very presence had created the accessibility problem were rudely shocked by two things.

First was the messy way the paralytic's friends solved the problem. Then came Jesus' completely unexpected reaction. When Jesus saw their faith [plural] emphasizing the four friends' role in the healing, He said, "Take heart, son; your sins are forgiven." Who said anything about sins? The religious began to whisper and in typical fashion, the experts started arguing. Jesus hushed the debate with words that seemed to sum up His general attitude toward physical healing, "Which is easier, to say to the paralytic, 'Your sins are forgiven,' or to say 'Get up, take your mat and walk'?"[2]

Apparently, Jesus enjoyed the interruption that day and loved the faith that was displayed by four healthy human beings, who cared so much about their friend that they were prepared to pay for a new roof, and possibly suffer the shame and humiliation of being mocked by the people and rejected by Christ.

Can you imagine a house filled with observers, not attending because of their need to hear the words of God, but to test His knowledge to see if it lines up with their creed? They were blocking the only way for a sick man to get a glimpse of this living Word on earth. So they fashioned their own way and caught His attention. One of the things that impressed Christ more than anything was their love for their friend. The one thing that we've failed to understand is that God created man for one main reason—friendship.

During His earthly ministry, Christ said these words to His disciples, "*No longer do I call you servants...but I have called you friends*" (John 15:15). The word used for friends in the Greek is *philos* or *philogos*, which means "someone to talk to" or "someone close to talk to."[3] God created you and I *to talk to*. He's not the problem, we are. He never ran from Adam and Eve, they ran from Him because of their perception of Him.

I see the paralytic as the people in the world—in pain and afraid. They don't know how to come through the front door of a church, so they find Him in another way. It's unorthodox, desperate, and in the midst of flying clay and dust they make their way to the Door and receive.

People in general are hungry to hear God speak to them. They've heard interpretations of His Word and would like to find out themselves. Once you understand the "friendship" aspect of your relationship with God, you will easily hear Him when He whispers or speaks audibly. You will recognize Him in certain deeds whether through people, the elements, His creation, or even through miserable circumstances. Whenever you are in trouble or hurting, look for Him, and if religion has cluttered the only way to Him, make a way, *make a hole in the roof to get to the Door!*

Presidential Visit

In the early years of my life, I heard things from within that I struggled to believe, and I was so hard on myself and self-prejudiced. I was not, after all, the neat and well-groomed boy whom everyone adored. I was rough and unruly, and I didn't fit into the role of a "spiritual leader."

I told some of my peers that I'd had a vision of myself counseling presidents and kings, and they ridiculed me. "Oh, you are going to the White House? 10 Downing Street?" they laughed as I tried to convince them that I had no doubt of the position I would be in. Why? Because God showed me where I would be one day.

They mocked me and called me a crazy fool. Many times I walked away because I feared that they were right.

My dream continued, and I enjoyed the imaginations. But my spiritual leaders told me that the imagination was an evil force. I would lay my head down on my pillow in the humble bedroom of my home in Uitenhage, South Africa, and dream of the day when I would stand before presidents and rulers of the world. My early wake-up call would bring me back to reality; I had to get up for work.

At the time, I was working at the Volkswagen factory because I had abandoned my musical career when I became a Christian. One day at work, I received a message from my supervisor's assistant. The director had come to meet with him, and they needed me to get a note to the company's chief executive officer who was in the meeting with them. The assistant told me the message, and I wrote it down and took it into the office where they were meeting.

I returned to my post, and noticed through the glass that they were passing my note around. They were examining it and passing it back and forth. Suddenly, they motioned for me to join them and asked, "Whose handwriting is this?" I cautiously told them that I had written it. After a pause, one of the directors said, "This is not the handwriting of a storekeeper, this is the handwriting of an executive!" They actually promoted me the next day. My handwriting is unique, and very different, and it represents my personality. God worked in strange ways to get me to the place where I was called to be.

Eventually, my family and I moved to the United States, after years of traveling and hardship. It wasn't an easy life for a long time, but I kept the dream in my heart. During very humiliating and difficult times, I would always talk about my meeting with presidents and great leaders. People looked at me as if I was crazy, and, yes, I was. I believed it myself.

Many years ago, I told my friend and travel companion, Bishop Babin, that he would accompany me to the White House and that he would meet presidents with me. Since then, he has been to the White House with me a number of times and personally met presidents with me.

One morning, during a particularly difficult period in our lives as a family, I had been working in Nashville, Tennessee, struggling to make ends meet, when I felt the Spirit telling me to prepare myself for a presidential visit. I was skeptical and very doubtful because of the difficulties we were facing at the time.

During the summer of that year, my son was falsely accused of trying to blow up his school when he was caught playing with a combustible substance, as many young boys have done in their youth, including myself. Many lies were told, and it escalated into an unbearable situation. We felt as though we were going through hell. I don't think I have ever been through something as rough, as we faced legal battles and the arraignment of my son, who was only 13 years of age at the time. Eventually it blew over, and even though we were seen as guilty, I heard something from God, "Now is the time for you to be promoted." I thought, "I wonder how this is going to happen?"

Later in the day, my long-time event coordinator and dear friend of the family, Debbie Aurin, called me regarding an invitation. Debbie knows well that I have declined many invitations, unless I have a revelation or the word to inspire and help someone.

She had received a call from a certain political party official, asking if I had a word or a prediction for this particular president. I was stunned. I had met a few presidents, and future presidents, but this was very important. I answered positively. Debbie said, "Prophet, are you sure?" Usually I don't respond as quickly. I needed a few hours to ponder, as Debbie well knows, so I told her I'd call back. I did. A few days later, I received the confirmation that I was cleared to meet the president in a private setting. We were frantic because we were in the worst place financially that we had ever been in.

The morning I was to fly out to meet him, I was going to wear a handsome suit that I had saved money to buy. I would be ready to present the word that God had given me. I awoke at 4:30 A.M. to dress and prepare for the flight and the meeting. As I was dressing, one of the dress shirt buttons broke, and I suddenly tore the shirt off my body. I wasn't going to struggle with this expensive and uncomfortable shirt, so I put on a jacket and black jeans and went off to meet with him feeling much more comfortable. It felt right.

As I waited around with a few important people, I began to ponder my dream in 1979. This was actually about to happen, and I was suddenly overwhelmed. What was I really going to say to him? I knew that he was going to be re-elected, and I had already predicted it before 5,000 people the Sunday before.

About ten minutes later, my friend Bishop Babin went into the room and informed the president who I was, in actuality, and what I had predicted. Then the bishop handed the president a scroll that contained my prediction for him. When I have something to say to dignitaries or celebrities, I always scribe the words in my own handwriting on beautiful paper as a reminder of the time long ago when I was promoted from a lowly desk clerk to an executive position, simply because of my handwriting, and to remind me of the skeptics who ridiculed me for simply listening to God.

It was very important for Bishop Babin to prepare the president, because the name "prophet" has been misappropriated to such a degree that most presidents would find it risky to be in the company of a prophet, especially when there were Fortune 500 CEOs and "normal" people right outside the door. I was summoned in and stood before the president of the United States of America. I presented the word to him and told him that he would be re-elected without a doubt. He was very open, and after I had shared my revelation with him, he said, "Thank you for the prophecy, and please pray for me and my family." Then something unusual happened. I had shaken his hand, taken a photo with him, and as I was leaving he grabbed my hand and said, "Thank you. Never stop prophesying, never stop prophesying." It was as if he was giving me an endorsement with a courageous, encouraging word.

He had no idea how deeply this touched me. A religious leader had just written to me the week before, telling me that I was to "stop prophesying" because I was a "false prophet," and that he represented a few other Full Gospel leaders. This was extremely hurtful to me. You expect this from your enemies but not from those who are supposedly in the field with you. However, here I was, receiving an endorsement from the highest office in the land. Suddenly, I realized that I was seeing another prophecy come to pass before my eyes.

Nothing is easy after the dream. I was accused and lied about. This is nothing unusual, but it affected me, and so I had to believe what I had seen was reality in advance. We had to struggle through many different city-living circumstances and cultural battles before the dream's reality came to pass. In the end, it happened and continues to happen. When God speaks to you, doors that were open, close, and closed doors open. The Law of Attraction is implemented and people are drawn to you to grant favor, and yes, unfortunately, to insult you in order to stop you.

Winston Churchill, prime minister of Great Britain during World War II, said; "Never give up, never give up, never give up." He should know, having been called "crazy" for facing Nazi Germany. *Never give up!*

No matter how difficult the circumstances became for me during the emergence of the dream, one thing I strongly grasped to was the fact that when I heard God speak to me, I also caught a glimpse of my future. I had seen myself in the future, and this was the greatest strength to me because I was able to make an adjustment to the present. When you hear God, your entire being is placed on hold for a while, or suspended, due to the fact that you are in an eternal state of existence; this means that you can see past, present, and future at once. Once I saw what only God can show a human being—the future—I could make corrections to my present state of being and change things so that I was prepared and ready for the next phase of my life.

When you see "you" in the future, then the future is (placed) inside of you; *a particular portion of space is placed in you.* This portion of space is the future, and once it's in you, **you cannot but live to get there!** You will defy insults, rejection and deplorable circumstances and survive anything *because something inside of you is driving you, instead of something outside of you drawing you.* Once the future is in you, the Law of Attraction is implemented and people are drawn to you and they cannot explain it. It's mysterious, alluring, and fascinating; it's something they're not familiar with—it's God: unexplained, pure, and unscathed by human vernacular.

My life is filled with all kinds of "moments." Most of the time, I can't explain it, and those around me are drawn into this magnificent, chaotic world that surrounds me. They love it, yet at times they run from it because it's so unexplainable. Their world changes, and their perception changes, and the contagious bug called "crazy" is caught, and it spreads like wildfire.

Have you caught "crazy"? If so, you will be looking at mountains as if they were molehills and at giants as if they were midgets; your perception of human beings will change, and a force of enthusiasm will sweep people off their feet—*the finale*—**God's love!**

Let's go crazy!

ENDNOTES

1.   Philip Yancey, *The Jesus I Never Knew*, (Grand Rapids, MI: Zondervan, 1995).

2.   *Ibid.*

MINISTRY PAGE

For more information about Kim Clement call us toll-free at 866-546-4366 or visit us online today at www.KIM-CLEMENT.COM. There you will find a complete listing of prophetic resources that can enrich your life and help you learn to hear the voice of God. Watch Kim's latest video webcast and check Kim's current television broadcast schedule. Also, get Kim's latest full-color digital newsletters, download the latest high-quality MP3 messages and music for your IPOD, get Kim's latest Schedule updates, and read the latest prophetic words that Kim has given that may impact your family, your business, your ministry, and your Nation.

Write to us and request a product catalog at:

Prophetic Image Expressions
The Ministry of Kim Clement
P.O. Box 470529
Tulsa, OK 74147-9902

If you are in the Los Angeles area come visit
Kim at Secrets—
The House of the Prophet
www.secretshollywood.com.